PRACTICAL HANDBOOK

THE BEGINNER'S GUIDE TO
ROCK CLIMBING

PRACTICAL HANDBOOK

THE BEGINNER'S GUIDE TO
ROCK CLIMBING

MALCOLM CREASEY
WITH NIGEL SHEPHERD AND NEIL GRESHAM

LORENZ BOOKS

This edition published by Lorenz Books

Lorenz Books is an imprint of
Anness Publishing Limited
Hermes House
88-89 Blackfriars Road
London SE1 8HA

Published in the USA by Lorenz Books
Anness Publishing Inc., 27 West 20th Street, New York, NY 10011;
(800) 354-9657

This edition distributed in Canada by Raincoast Books
8680 Cambie Street, Vancouver, British Columbia V6P 6M9

A CIP catalogue record for this book is available from the British Library

Publisher: JOANNA LORENZ
Senior Editorial Manager: JUDITH SIMONS
Consultant and Project Editor: NEIL CHAMPION
Editor: MARIANO KÄLFORS
US Consultant: BOB DURAND
Designer: LISA TAI
Location Photographer: RAY WOOD
Studio Photographer: MARK DUNCALF
Illustrator: GEORGE MANLEY
Production Controller: DON CAMPANIELLO
Editorial Reader: DIANE ASHMORE

Also published as *An Introduction to Rock Climbing* and as
part of a larger compendium, *The Complete Rock Climber*

Printed and bound in China

1 3 5 7 9 10 8 6 4 2

Photo credits. © Malcolm Creasey: pages 5, 72 t, 104 and 117. © Alex Gillespie: page, 90 b. © Neil Gresham: pages 13 tl,
26. © Nigel Shepherd: pages 34 l, 47 l r, 48 t, 49 b. © David Simmonite: pages 15 t b, 91 b. © Paul Twomey: page 14 t.
© Ray Wood: pages 2 tl cl bl, 3, 7, 9, 10, 11 tl tr b, 12 br, 14 b, 18 bl, 21 tr cr, 33 b, 34, 35 tl, 39 t, 50, 55 r, 60 l r, 67 l r, 68, 70 l,
73 tl tr, 74, 75 r, 78 l, 93 t, 96 b, 102 tl, 106.

CONTENTS

INTRODUCTION

Rock climbing today is a complex sport, complete with its own vocabulary and equipment that have come about over decades of experimentation. It has for many years been one of the fastest growing leisure activities, involving millions of people worldwide. From its relatively simple beginnings in Victorian Britain and Europe, it has evolved into a vast game with many facets, defying easy definition and categorization. Around it there has developed a mass of special terms describing particular aspects of the sport (bouldering, soloing, sport climbing, traditional climbing, competition climbing, and so on); pieces of equipment (harness, karabiner, quickdraws, belay devices, rock shoes); moves (dyno, Egyptian, layback, mantleshelf); and particular holds and how to use them (sloper, off-width, crimp, jam). Even the environment in which the sport takes place has changed and developed – from the original mountain gullies and ridges, to the harder rock walls and faces, the smaller outcrops of rock closer to cities, towns and roads, and finally to the totally modern phenomenon of the indoor climbing wall.

Rock climbing has always been a sport with few rules, and this remains the case today. It has also carried with it from its earliest days the element of risk. Personal safety at an indoor climbing wall is one thing, but out on the crags or in the mountains it is certainly another. Personal judgement when weighing up the degree of risk involved in doing a particular climb is still an important aspect of being a competent rock climber. To some degree, these things set climbing apart from most other sports, which have set rules, generally carry far less objective risk, and do not exact such a high payment for poor judgement and decision making.

There are many skills to be learned before anyone can claim to be a confident and competent all-round rock climber. These encompass the physical, technical and mental strengths that the sport draws on. The process of gaining new skills in each of these areas never stops. That is one of the great things about the climbing game. Even a highly experienced professional mountain guide cannot claim to know it all! But above all, the sport should bring enjoyment and fulfilment to those who practise it. Each day on the rock should bring a little more fun, an opportunity to learn new skills, and a good reason to explore unknown territory, either close at hand or far away. The challenges that you may choose to accept are always personal ones – they relate to your physical ability and to your own level of risk acceptance. At whatever level you choose to climb, this book will provide you with the essential knowledge to apply safe practice and to gain that all-important experience in this multi-faceted sport.

Above and opposite: *These are just two facets of rock climbing today, the indoor environment differing considerably in both physical and mental approach from the outdoor one.*

1

A MODERN VIEW

When rock climbing as an independent past-time grew out of the greater game of mountaineering, the idea was simple: climb from the bottom of a cliff to the top, placing as much protective equipment as possible along the way. The concept still holds today to some extent, but to understand the modern sport of rock climbing, it helps to bear in mind that as an expanding global pursuit the rules that govern it are simple: there are none. Instead, various ethics and codes of practice have sprung up in tandem with the sport's evolution. For the newly initiated, getting to grips with the various issues surrounding the sport, from grading debates to climbing etiquette, can be a struggle. This chapter aims to provide a useful insight into some of these concerns.

Opposite: *To many rock climbers this is the ultimate challenge, where high alpine terrain has to be climbed quickly before bad weather turns it into a fight for survival. Others, who have no desire for the high mountains, can still enjoy the pleasures that rock climbing brings on less hazardous terrain far from the mountain environment.*

Commercialization

While the spirit of fun and fair play that was generated by the early pioneers of rock climbing is still very much alive today, the rapid force of change is re-shaping the cutting edge of the sport. Gone is the light-hearted touch; the modern extreme climber is unashamedly competitive and dedicated. As standards rise and the level of commercialization in climbing increases, it is common practice for those at the top end to take their training and preparation as seriously as any Olympic athlete. The lure of lucrative sponsorship deals and competition prize money now make it possible for a few climbers to make a comfortable living from their sport. Far from being just a hobby, the addictiveness of climbing has a habit of turning into a full-blown obsession, even for those who operate at a more modest level. Heated debates rage over grades and ethical practices, often spilling over on to the pages of the climbing magazines.

SPECIALIZATION

Perhaps the most notable characteristic of modern climbing is the rate at which it has become increasingly specialized. It is now possible for two different people who would categorize themselves as rock climbers to be participating in very different sports. Just as the term "runner" says nothing about whether an individual is a sprinter or runs marathons, the term "rock climber" has become a generalization that is rendered almost obsolete. Whether it is sport climbing, big-wall aiding, free soloing, competitions or bold traditional climbing, the ethics are different, the climbing style is different and the attitudes towards training and preparation could not be more diverse.

WORLD GRADING SYSTEMS

There are now in excess of ten different grading systems used worldwide today to categorize the difficulty of different types of rock climbing. The most popular systems are:

△ *Gravediggers, E8 (6c), North Wales – a route which symbolizes the modern trend for ascending hard, traditionally protected routes using the type of tactics that are normally associated with sport climbing.*

● WORLD GRADING SYSTEM

Britain	USA	Australia	France	UIAA*
Difficult	5.3	11	2	II
Very Difficult	5.4	12	3	III
Severe (4a)**	5.5	12/13	4	IV/IV+
Hard Severe (4b)	5.6	13/14	5	V-
Very Severe (4c)	5.7	15	5/5+	V
Hard Very Severe (5a)	5.8/9	16/17	5+	VI-
E1*** (5b)	5.10a/b	18/19	6a/6a+	VI/VI+
E2 (5c)	5.10c/d	20/21	6b/6b+	VII-/VII
E3 (6a)	5.11a/b/c	22/23/24	6c/6c+/7a	VII+/VIII-

*   UIAA stands for Union Internationale des Associations d'Alpinistes.
**   The British technical grade is given in brackets. This shows how hard the hardest move on a climb will be.
*** E stands for Extreme!
The grades shown above are just a sample selection to illustrate equivalents. Grades in all countries are open-ended; they will continue to increase as long as people attempt harder climbs.

△ Bouldering, while providing a great way to hone your skills for longer rock climbs, has now become a separate sport in its own right.

△ With the aid of bolt protection, sport routes provide the opportunity to focus on the physical and technical challenges of climbing.

△ Top roping on an indoor leading wall: a convenient way of staying in shape during the off-season or an independent sport if you are a competition climber.

(for free climbing) French, British, German, USA, Australian, Norwegian; (for aid climbing) the "A" grades or USA big-wall grades; (for mountaineering-style rock routes) Alpine or UIAA; and (for bouldering) the "B" system, "V" system and Fontainebleau grades.

To the novice climber who is struggling to get to grips with grading in their own country, the thought of travelling abroad and having to tackle all these various systems can be daunting. Fortunately, most guidebooks offer user-friendly conversion tables to help you know what you are letting yourself in for.

As climbing becomes more advanced and specialized, grading systems have adapted and evolved to express the varying nature of the objective difficulties that may be encountered on a particular climb. For example, the early British system used a simple adjectival grade to make an overall assessment of the climb: Moderate (Mod), Difficult (Diff), Severe (S), Very Severe (VS), Extremely Severe (XS). When it was first developed, no climber could possibly have conceived the need for a grade any harder than XS, but it was soon realized that the Extremely Severe grades would need to be extended. They now range from E1 up to E10 at the time of writing. These British

descriptive grades would embrace all aspects of overall climbing difficulty, including strenuousness, seriousness, availability of protection, level of commitment required, presence of hazards such as loose rock, and so on. However, concurrent with the development of the "E" grades was the realization that this system was still incapable of differentiating between the overall difficulty of a climb and the technical difficulty of its hardest move.

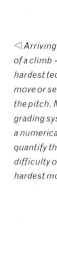

◁ Arriving at the crux of a climb – this is the hardest technical move or sequence on the pitch. Modern grading systems use a numerical grade to quantify the technical difficulty of the hardest move.

Grade and ethical debates

By definition, grading is a subjective issue and differences between the heights, builds, climbing styles and opinions of individuals make it impossible to have an entirely standardized system. The main discrepancy that crops up time and again in grading debates is the breadth of each grade and the arbitrary points at which grades seem to overlap. For this reason, climbers are often reluctant to commit themselves and state a definitive grade for a particular route, preferring instead to take the safe option of saying, for example, "Maybe hard French 6c or easy 6c+". Grading first ascents can be especially difficult, as new routers must bear in mind that

most routes clean up (by the removal of dirt, lichen and loose holds) after repeat traffic. In addition, the first ascentionist must cope with the increased psychological pressure from not knowing whether a climb is possible or how hard it will be. A combination of these factors may lead to some new routes being downgraded by as much as two or three grades after repeat ascents.

ETHICAL CONTROVERSIES

Inherently linked with the issue of grading is the complicated and highly contentious issue of the style in which an ascent is made. There is no disputing the fact that when rock climbing evolved as a break-off sport from mountaineering, the idea was to start at the bottom of a cliff and climb it to the top, placing all protection during the ascent and with no prior knowledge of the route. It seems clear and, indeed, if everyone adhered to this simple code there would be no need for ethical debate. The problem comes when individuals reach their own physical and mental limits in climbing using the traditional ethic, but still desire to push things further. At this point it always seems easier to bend the rules rather than spend years of training in an attempt to improve your skills further. Then, with the passage of time, as more and more climbers bend the rules in a similar manner, a new code of practice becomes accepted. It was an inevitable consequence that the use of pre-placed protection (including bolts), pre-inspection of climbs by abseil (rappel), and even top-rope rehearsal prior to the lead would become commonplace if harder routes were to be ascended. The open-minded will embrace both the old (on-sight) style and the new (pre-rehearsed) style.

▷ *Some climbers still bitterly dispute the arrival of so-called modern ethics, arguing that they merely serve to bring the climbs down to the level of the climber.*

▽ *An in situ hanger bolt – the answer to the safe future of climbing or the death of long-standing ethics and traditions?*

△ Free soloing is arguably the purest form of climbing, though with the most serious consequences for failure.

△ A sea-cliff route that can only be reached by abseil (rappel) automatically carries with it a level of seriousness and commitment.

△ A traditional crag where the bolt-free ethic preserves the adventurous character of mountain rock climbing.

● CLIMBING TERMS

Traditional climbing Climbing that puts emphasis on traditional values. This mainly centres on climbing a route using leader-placed protection, which is removed by the second climber, and on climbing without rehearsing or pre-inspecting the route.

Sport climbing A style of climbing that uses bolts as the main form of protection, allowing the climber to concentrate on technique and hard moves.

Big-wall climbing Climbing on big walls that usually take several days to complete. Special techniques, such as aid climbing, sack hauling, and sleeping on portaledges, have all been developed to support this style of climbing.

Aid climbing Climbing that is carried out using pegs (pitons), nuts and other equipment to directly help an ascent, as opposed to being used solely for protection. Equipment can be pulled on or stood in to assist ascent. Aid climbing is usually practised when time is short or where the route is too hard to be climbed in a purer style.

Free climbing Climbing that makes use of natural hand and foot holds only, using the rope and protection only as back-up. Contrast this with aid climbing, in which equipment is used to pull on or stand in to assist ascent.

Free soloing Climbing without ropes or any form of protection. A fall while soloing may be fatal.

Bouldering A form of soloing, but the climber reaches no greater height than they can reasonably safely fall from. It is most often carried out on boulders around 3m–5m (10ft–16ft) high.

Route preparation practices

△ △ *Extreme, traditionally protected routes are still made by modern climbers today.*

The question of which tactics are considered acceptable in the preparation of a new route by a first ascentionist is another highly contentious issue in climbing. If you take the standpoint that all routes should be attempted on-sight, then once again there is no need for discussion. Some incredible new lines have been climbed from the ground up, often with holds being brushed and loose rock being prized off while leading. However, the practicalities of new routing mean that most climbers will settle for a compromise and abseil (rappel) the line first to clean it and make an assessment of available protection. There are, of course, environmental implications to this procedure and excessive "gardening" may present a threat to rare flora or damage softer rocks if a hard brush is over-used. Worse still and now deemed as highly unacceptable is the use of a chisel or drill to improve or manufacture holds. Sadly, chipping has become a widespread practice in certain countries which have failed to appreciate their rock as a non-renewable resource. Climbing is still such a young sport and nobody is entitled to make the assumption that a piece of rock is unclimbable. Future generations of more talented climbers may succeed!

A SPORT WITHOUT RULES

The beauty of climbing has always been that it has no rules and yet it is this very fact that opens the floodgates to an endless list of ethical issues. Of course, it is up to the individual to take their own personal standpoint, provided it does not jeopardize the activities

◁ *With a battery-powered cordless drill, expansion bolts can be placed in a matter of minutes on suitable rock.*

of other climbers. While it is easy to be drawn into debates concerning those practices that are on the borderline of ethical acceptability, hopefully there is no further contention over the biggest ethical crimes.

A more complicated issue is whether glue or epoxy resins should be considered acceptable for the purpose of stabilizing loose rock. Some would argue that this is tolerable, provided that the hold is not improved and that the presence of the glue is highly discrete. Other nations have an almost free-for-all attitude to this type of issue and if a hold breaks off they simply bolt an artificial resin hold on in its place, perhaps smearing glue over it to make it less of an eyesore. If the distinction between indoor and outdoor climbing is to remain, these practices are to be condemned.

USING PEGS (PITONS) AND BOLTS

Another important issue faced by prospective new routers is whether to make use of various forms of fixed or in-situ protection, namely pegs (pitons) or bolts. The argument in favour of pegs is that their placement is still very much governed by the availability of natural cracks and that they cause less damage to the rock than bolts. However, any aid climber knows that the repeated placement and removal of pegs eventually causes hairline seams to be widened into finger cracks. The alternative is for them to be left in place, but here there is the risk that they will corrode away and become highly dangerous. For these reasons many modern free climbers will choose not to place pegs but climb without protection, creating a climb with a higher overall level of seriousness.

With regards to the placement of expansion bolts using either a battery-powered cordless

△ An abseil (rappel) inspection of a climb will provide an abundance of information which may make a subsequent ascent less taxing.

● STYLES OF ASCENT

On-sight The purest form of traditional ascent, where the climber starts from the bottom and climbs to the top in one push with no falls, placing all protection on the lead and with no prior knowledge of the intricacies of the climb.

Flash (beta flash) As with on-sight but using prior knowledge of moves, protection or both.

Ground-up (yo-yo) This is essentially a failed on-sight ascent where the climber falls, lowers to the ground and then either pulls the ropes through or, alternatively, top-ropes back up to their high point, either to complete the climb or repeat the same process until eventually the route succumbs.

Pre-inspection This ethic may be applied to traditional or sport climbs by making a prior abseil (rappel) inspection of a climb to clean or examine holds, or assess protection opportunities. If any moves are practised during the abseil then the ascent should be classified as a redpoint.

Redpoint A term developed for sport climbing to describe the process of repeatedly practising the moves of a climb (either by top-rope or repeated leader falls) before eventually completing it in one push, leading, clipping all protection and without falls.

Headpoint A term coined to describe the use of redpointing tactics to ascend bold, naturally protected climbs.

Day ascent The ethical ideal for multipitch free routes. It is common for those routes, which were first climbed with the use of fixed ropes over several days, to be attempted in a day by repeat ascentionists.

drill or a hand drill, this is perhaps the most over-scrutinized ethical issue in climbing. Countries such as France or Spain accept bolting universally, which means that the use of traditional forms of protection has all but died out, except in high mountainous regions. Countries such as Britain held out against the overwhelming pressure for bolting and then eventually succumbed to the use of bolts in certain designated areas. Other countries, such as the United States and Norway, have a policy of minimal bolting on certain crags, with crack-lines tending to be climbed on natural protection and the blank faces between them often being equipped with bolts. Needless to say it is the type of rock that tends to have the greatest influence on the decision to use bolts. Smoother, less fractured rocks such as limestone offer far less in the way of natural protection and hence become obvious targets for bolting. Any climber who is uncertain of a national policy on fixed protection is advised to consult their governing associations (or relevant guidebooks) before they equip a new line.

◁ Controversy over bolts: these old ring bolts have been chopped, being deemed out of place in an area that maintains a long tradition of adventure climbing.

GETTING STARTED

There are many ways in which you can get started in the sport of rock climbing. Today, one of the most popular is to find an indoor climbing wall. Many towns and cities have climbing clubs, which will welcome new members. This is an ideal way to benefit from the experience of other members. Outdoor centres run courses on climbing and safe practice. Whichever route you choose, you will need to consider the equipment you buy and, once on the rock, your climbing technique. This chapter will help you in these first steps, pointing you in the direction of those all-important early experiences.

Opposite: *Rock climbing is an exciting and demanding sport. Developing good technique early on will stand anyone in good stead for future, harder climbs.*

Choosing clothing

Clothing should be chosen according to the environment in which you intend to climb. What you wear in winter on a heated indoor climbing wall might also be what you wear outside in summer on a hot day – shorts and a t-shirt. However, climbing outside carries an element of uncertainty not found indoors – that of the weather and its changeable nature. It is always wise to carry layers of clothing, providing warmth (fleece or wool), windproof protection and maybe even waterproof protection. Today there is an enormous choice of clothing, covering every conceivable situation and designed to fit all shapes and sizes. Most manufacturers offer key lines in both male and female designs. Consider carefully what you require your clothing for. That way, you will avoid wasting your money.

FABRICS

There are no rights and wrongs about what you should wear to climb in. Personal preference will influence you. However, some fabrics are better than others for different situations. For example, cotton is comfortable and absorbs sweat, but it is not hardwearing, does not dry quickly and does not keep you warm. You might choose it if you are climbing indoors. Man-made fabrics, such as polyester and

◁ It is important to dress for the occasion – and of course with some style! In hot climates, being cool and comfortable will enhance enjoyment.

▷ A breezy day by the sea or on a mountain crag may require full body cover, but be sure that what you wear is light and unrestrictive.

nylon, are hardwearing and dry quickly. Some wick sweat away from your skin. You might choose them when climbing outdoors. Fleece is a fine example of such a fabric and is available in many guises.

If you like tight-fitting clothes, make sure they stretch. Modern fabrics allow manufacturers to be inventive with design, style and variety. Lycra fabrics are perhaps the stretchiest of all; garments fit snugly around the body but do not restrict movement in any way. Lycra in itself is not hardwearing and is usually mixed with other fabrics to provide durability. Out on the crags, walls and boulders, clothing is subject to constant abrasion, which makes this an important consideration.

Close-fitting clothing, particularly fleece, can be quite clammy, especially on hot, sunny days or when you are working hard. It will feel uncomfortable and cause overheating, which saps valuable energy. A great many climbers prefer looser clothing.

◁ For indoor climbing or outside on warm sunny days, light clothing is perfectly adequate, though you'll certainly have to carry something warmer as well when outdoors.

▽ For warmer wear, if you choose the "baggy" look make sure that clothing doesn't obstruct gear handling. Stretch fleece wear is warm and snug-fitting for a more "sporty" look.

● MOISTURE CONTROL

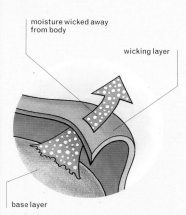

moisture wicked away from body

wicking layer

base layer

△ During any exertion, the body gives off moisture in the form of sweat. It is important to get rid of this, to avoid your body over-cooling once you stop working. Man-made fibres do this by wicking moisture away from the skin.

Choosing equipment

To begin climbing at its most basic level, that of bouldering (either indoors or out), you will need very few pieces of specialist equipment. To get the most out of the activity, you will need a pair of rock shoes and a chalk bag. You might also wish to wear a helmet when you start out on your climbing career. It is highly recommended that you do wear a helmet, but more experienced climbers will often choose not to. At the end of the day, it is a matter of personal preference, but there is no doubt that helmets have saved lives.

▷ *You can have plenty of fun with just a pair of rock shoes and a chalk bag. Equipment is expensive and to begin with you might seek to borrow from friends or to hire from professional outlets.*

ROCK SHOES

The choice of footwear depends entirely on your sphere of activity. If you choose to climb only on indoor walls and to boulder, a light and snug-fitting pair of slipper-style rock shoes is adequate. This type gives a high degree of sensitivity in feeling the holds on which you place your feet. This is advantageous to an experienced climber but the benefits may not be appreciated fully at a beginner level. Slipper-style shoes do not offer much in the way of support and protection for the feet, so if you intend to climb on more adventurous rock you will need to consider this factor and choose something more robust.

The sturdier and more supportive the shoe, the less sensitive it will be to standing on tiny edges or smearing holds. Fortunately, the greatest diversity of shoe design is found in the range of shoes intended for the widest application. As with clothing, not all styles or models will fit all shapes and sizes of feet. It is important to try on as many different shoes as you can. Even so, finding a shoe that is comfortable in the shop does not necessarily mean that it will be comfortable out on the crag. Climbing in hot conditions for hours at a time encourages

● LOOKING AFTER YOUR CLIMBING SHOES

Rock shoes are expensive. They will last longer and give better performance if you take a little time to look after them. Keep the soles clean by wiping them after use. This is especially important after using them outdoors, where grit, mud and sand can all stick to the rubber soles, detracting from their amazing friction properties. Always be sure to wipe them before setting off on a climb.

Rock shoes can be repaired by specialist companies once they start to wear out. This is done by replacing worn-out rands and toe caps, and also the sole, if necessary.

△ *A selection of footwear: two shoe styles, two boots and a slipper.*

feet to swell, and though shoes will stretch a little with use, they might become uncomfortably tight. Very painful feet are not usually conducive to pleasurable climbing experiences.

CHALK AND CHALK BAGS

The use of chalk to increase hand grip is widespread. Chalk absorbs moisture from the fingertips and allows the climber to hold on with greater confidence, which also means the climber endures that little bit longer. Chalk is available in block form and is broken into tiny pieces and carried on a waistband in a small pouch, called a chalk bag. This bag need only be big enough to get the fingers of one hand into at one time. Some indoor walls have banned the use of this type of chalk for reasons of health and cleanliness. Certainly if you fall upside down, a deluge of chalk dust is likely to fall on to your belayer and pollute the air. Chalk balls go some way to alleviating this problem. These are chalk-filled secure muslin (cheesecloth) bags that are simply kept in the chalk bag itself. When squeezed, chalk is released through small holes in the muslin. It is also possible to buy very large chalk bags intended for communal use.

CRASHMATS

If you get really serious about your bouldering you might want to consider acquiring a crashmat. There are a number of types available, some of which fold up into quite small packages and are easy to carry, yet still provide adequate cushioning.

▷ *All you need for sport climbing – shoes, harness, chalk bag, quickdraws and a rope.*

△ *A chalk bag and chalk ball.*

▷ *Bouldering is very much a social activity and though you may find that there will always be someone to "spot" you if you fall off, a crashmat is very reassuring if you are likely to land on your back.*

● HELMETS

There are many different types available commercially. Most are made from plastic or fibreglass, although some new designs have used the cycle helmet model and use very light polystyrene. Things to look out for are weight (most people prefer light helmets), durability (some designs will only take one knock and should then be retired), and fit. They are designed to take an impact from above (in the event of falling stones) and the sides. If a helmet does sustain a major impact, it should be replaced.

△ *A good all-purpose helmet.*

△ *An ill-fitting helmet.*

More equipment

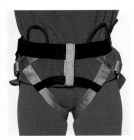

△ *A simple and inexpensive adjustable harness is fine for starting out.*

△ *A well-padded harness for rock climbing. This will be comfortable and provide plenty of gear loops for equipment.*

△ *A fully adjustable harness is preferable for all-round climbing use, including winter and alpine mountaineering.*

Climbing beyond bouldering implies the use of more equipment. You will need a rope, harness, belay device, screwgate or locking karabiner, and some quickdraws. This equipment will enable you to start climbing at an indoor wall and on sport routes outside. However, many walls have quickdraws already in place in bolts on the routes for leading and ropes for bottom-roping. You may also be able to hire rock shoes, harnesses and anything else you require.

CHOOSING A HARNESS

More than any other item of gear, harnesses present the widest variety of design and style. This can make it difficult to decide on the most suitable type for your chosen style of climbing. If you climb only on indoor walls and outdoors on sport climbs that are protected by in situ bolts, you will have little need for anything more sophisticated than the simplest and lightest harness available. For comfort, it is better to opt for a harness with a fixed-size waist belt and padded leg loops. You will not need to carry heavy equipment on the harness, nor are you likely to require it to fit over bulky clothing. However, if you plan to climb on high mountain routes, you might like to consider a fully adjustable harness. This will enable you to fit it over whatever clothing you need to wear.

BELAY DEVICES

The belay device and karabiner that you choose are likely to be suitable for almost any climbing situation, either indoors or outdoors, so consider carefully what you buy and you will certainly save money at a later date. However, some climbing walls stipulate the type of device that should be used. In Britain

this is rarely the case, but there are many indoor venues in other countries that insist on a device that has a "fail-safe" mechanism such as the Petzl Gri-Gri. Proper training in the safe operation of whatever device you use is essential and it is quite possible that on a first visit to an indoor wall you will be asked to demonstrate your belaying skills prior to being permitted to climb.

KARABINERS

A belay device needs a screwgate or "locking" karabiner, usually a HMS (or pear-shaped) one. This allows the rope to run smoothly through a belay device and lessens the chance of a tangle occurring or the rope jamming. Snaplink karabiners are used in quickdraws for speedy clipping – the rope goes into the bent gate.

◁ *A belay device with screwgate or locking karabiner.*

◁ *The Gri-Gri is a belay device with a fail-safe mechanism.*

▽ *A few quickdraws will allow you to lead sport climbs.*

ROPES

Ropes come in two main strengths: full (or single) and half (or double). A full rope can be used on its own, whereas a half rope must be used in conjunction with another half rope. Full ropes have traditionally been 11 mm in thickness (although today this has been reduced to 9.8 mm), and half ropes 9 mm in thickness. In terms of length, you can buy standard 45 m (148 ft), 50 m (164 ft), 55 m (180 ft) and even 60 m (197 ft) ropes. Obviously, the thicker and longer a rope, the heavier it will be.

You can also buy ropes that have been treated to repel water. These are useful for climbing outdoors but not necessary if you only climb indoors. This treatment inevitably puts the price of the rope up.

It is important to read the accompanying manufacturer's safety notes when you buy your rope. They will give a recommended life-span (dependent on how often you use it and how you take care of it), and how many heavy falls it could take.

Ropes are expensive and you may not feel inclined to use your best climbing rope on a climbing wall. The chances are that you will spend a great deal of time at the wall attempting routes that are beyond your ability and consequently might take numerous, though short, falls on to the rope. The longevity of a rope reduces considerably the more frequently it is subjected to a fall. Even short falls will stretch a rope and eventually its ability to

absorb shock will diminish. The ends of the rope will also be subjected to considerably greater wear and tear than the middle part. If you visit climbing walls regularly, say three or four times a week, and you can afford to, it is a good idea to buy a rope that is designed to be used exclusively for this purpose. Manufacturers now produce short ropes specifically to meet this market demand. If you have an old rope that has been retired from more serious use, you could also consider cutting out the worn bits and using that. Be certain though that there is still sufficient life in the rope to justify its continued use.

△ The accoutred climber. Buy what you need as you gain more experience. The rope is perhaps the single most expensive item of gear you will need but taking care of it will make it last for many years.

● CROSS-SECTION OF ROPE

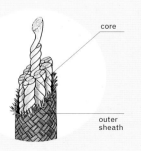

core

outer sheath

◁ Modern ropes are dynamic – they stretch. This property absorbs the energy of a fall. The inner core provides the greatest contribution to strength and elasticity, with the sheath acting as a protective cover.

△ A rope bag is useful for keeping the rope clean and for ease of carrying.

Why warm up?

THE MAIN MUSCLE GROUPS

FRONT VIEW OF MUSCLE GROUPS

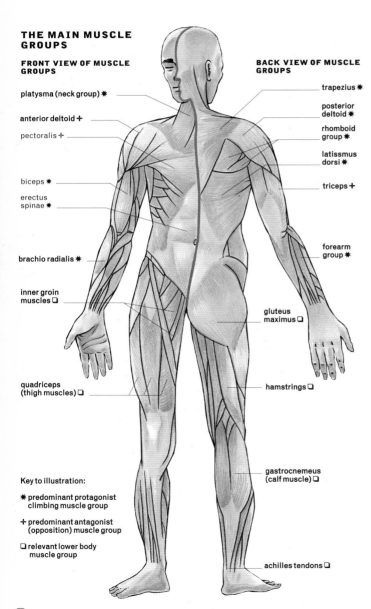

platysma (neck group) ✳

anterior deltoid +

pectoralis +

biceps ✳

erectus spinae ✳

brachio radialis ✳

inner groin muscles ❏

quadriceps (thigh muscles) ❏

BACK VIEW OF MUSCLE GROUPS

trapezius ✳

posterior deltoid ✳

rhomboid group ✳

latissmus dorsi ✳

triceps +

forearm group ✳

gluteus maximus ❏

hamstrings ❏

gastrocnemeus (calf muscle) ❏

achilles tendons ❏

Key to illustration:

✳ predominant protagonist climbing muscle group

+ predominant antagonist (opposition) muscle group

❏ relevant lower body muscle group

Whether you are about to attempt your very first climb or compete in the final of a top international competition, the importance of warming up for climbing cannot be stressed enough. Most climbers are notoriously lazy when it comes to correct preparation practices; after all, if you don't take climbing that seriously, then why should you prepare for it as if it were an athletic sport? Climbing is one of the most punishing activities ever invented for joints and connective tissues, and yet many of its participants still seem to hold the belief that injury is something that only happens to other people. Equally surprising are the numbers who have suffered the odd tweaked tendon or muscle and yet completely fail to learn from their previous mistakes. Of course, there are other factors, aside from warming up, that will have some influence on your ability to avoid injury: the amount of rest you take between climbs or climbing days, your sleep patterns and your nutritional intake, to name but a few. But in the short term, the most important variable will be the effectiveness of your pre-climbing preparation routine.

IMPROVE YOUR CLIMBING

If the threat of injury is not a good enough incentive, then the other main reason to warm up is that it helps you to climb better. We all know how it feels to arrive at work having just fallen out of bed – mental and physical attunement take their time and you simply cannot expect your muscles to be able to pull their hardest or be smooth and co-ordinated if you

◁ Climbing puts tremendous stress on muscles and joints. It is worth knowing a little about your anatomy to help avoid injury.

△ *Build up gradually before launching into steep, dynamic climbing.*

jump from a sedentary state straight into your hardest climb or boulder problem. A warm-up routine also gives you sufficient time to filter out the cluttered chaotic thoughts generated by your work or social schedule, and focus in on the task of climbing.

A SYSTEMATIC APPROACH

How many times at the crag or climbing wall have you seen people arrive looking as if they lack direction? Then while getting changed or chatting to a friend they will go through the motions of a warm-up by performing a few violent helicopter-style arm circles, yank their fingers backwards and forwards and then finish with a half-hearted bouncing touch of the toes? The irony is that some of the bizarre and extreme forms of so-called warm-up that you occasionally witness are potentially more damaging than climbing itself! It is very important to learn safe practices from the very start and to adopt a consistent approach to warming up every time you climb. After all, the warm-up is an ideal time to gauge how good you are feeling, and whether or not you have recovered from your previous climbing session. Climbers

△ *Even on remote mountain crags, it pays to have a quick boulder around before commencing a longer, more committed climb.*

◁ *It may help your warm-up routine to have a few practice routes that you know well. Climbing them will indicate how in-tune and warmed-up you really are.*

who are well in tune with their warm-up will use a series of benchmark exercises as a gauge for how hard they should push themselves throughout the remainder of the session proper. It is also worth taking the time to practise a few standard routine warm-up routes or problems at your regular climbing venues. These will also give clues as to how well you are performing on a particular day.

Progression

▽ Your warm-up will play a vital role in the outcome of a steep strenuous ascent such as this 8a sport climb.

The most important thing about a warm-up is that it must introduce increasing overload to the relevant climbing muscle groups in a gradual and controlled manner over a reasonable time period. To go "too hard too soon" is to ruin your warm-up. You will know when you have done this by the fact that you won't climb anything harder than your so-called warm-up route or boulder problem in the rest of the session. If you are at a crag that has no suitable easy routes and you are forced to warm up on something difficult, make yourself stop intermittently and take rests between individual moves (if a top rope or the protection permits) and treat the exercise as if you were warming up for bouldering. Although less desirable, this is far better than jumping straight on something hard and heading for the inevitable burn-out. If you are pushed for time, then you may be able to cut out certain less relevant parts of your warm-up routine. However, the progressive build-up of effort must always stay if you are to avoid injury, even if it means less climbing time as a result.

SPECIFICITY

Certain core elements of your warm-up must be consistent, while others should vary according to the specific type of climbing that you are about to do. It may sound obvious, but why perform lots of laborious leg stretches if you only plan to go on a steep bouldering wall or fingerboard board? However, if you are about to attempt a leg-contorting slab route you will need to put more time into calf, thigh and groin stretches. It is also vital to make your warm-up intensity-specific. Use easy boulder problems to warm up for bouldering or power-training sessions and use easy traverses, circuits or routes to prepare for longer endurance climbing.

THE FOUR-POINT WARM-UP GUIDE

This covers the core areas of a suggested warm-up routine for climbing. It is laid out in

△ Jogging on the spot provides a good way of raising your pulse at the beginning of your warm-up session.

▷ Some light climbing, where careful attention is paid to form and control, should always precede more strenuous climbing.

the order in which you should do them, to get the most out of your warm-up. The stages are:

① Pulse raiser
② General mobility
③ Specific stretching
④ Progressive climbing build-up

PULSE RAISER

If you are slogging up a steep hill to reach a distant mountain crag, then you can happily forget this first stage. But if you are stepping out of your car to the foot of a roadside sport climbing venue or a climbing wall, then you will need to do something to get your heart and lungs going before you attempt to do any stretching, let alone climbing. By raising your pulse for approximately 3–5 minutes, with a quick jog, skip or some on-the-spot style exercises, you will increase overall blood flow, warm the muscles and generally trigger your body into exercise mode. This vital part of the warm-up also serves to soften joint cartilage in preparation for the impacts of strenuous exercise.

GENERAL MOBILITY

Before you attempt to stretch, it pays to do some controlled circular movements. For example, both the shoulders and hips can be gently rotated to warm the joints up, and to get your muscles, tendons and joints used to working through a full range of motion. To save time, you can combine these with some finger clenches, either with or without the use of a wrist exerciser. Violent swinging movements are definitely out – especially when the spine is involved. Use a smooth "front-crawl"-style swimming action for your arms.

Upper body stretches

As an overall rule your core stretches, which should be common to every climbing session, are the fingers and forearms, elbow tendon insertions, shoulders and neck. For steep rock, pay particular attention to your back and sides, and for lower angled rock, make sure you go through your leg stretches.

FINGER STRETCHES

First perform some finger clenches, either with or without a grip exerciser. Then carefully work through each individual finger and thumb joint, stretching them both ways for approximately 6–8 seconds and up to three times each. Apply even, progressive pressure with no sharp tugging. You can maybe do this on the journey to the crag or wall to save time.

△ Finger clenches with or without a grip exerciser will develop finger and overall hand strength.

△ The thumb stretch.

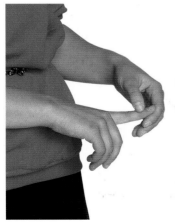

△ First joint finger stretch.

△ Second joint finger stretch.

△ Third joint finger stretch.

ELBOW AND FOREARM STRETCH

Hold one arm out straight in front of you, clasp the fingers with your spare hand and bend your wrist and fingers back, so as to take up the tension on the flexor tendon insertion to the elbow. Hold for 8–12 seconds and repeat three times for each arm.

SHOULDER STRETCHES

Stand upright, grasp your elbow and bring your upper arm behind your head, applying gentle downward pressure to stretch the deltoid muscles. Then hold your arm out straight in front of you and pull it sideways across your body. Hold each stretch for 8–12 seconds and repeat three times.

◁ Forearm stretch.

△ Shoulder stretch (1).

△ Shoulder stretch (2).

NECK STRETCH

Stand or sit upright, then gently bend your neck to one side, back to the centre and then to the other side, to the front and then to the back, always returning to the centre first each time. Do not rotate your neck.

BACK STRETCHES

For your lats (the large wing-like muscles down your sides), stand legs apart and slightly bent, then lean sideways stretching the leading arm over your head so as to feel the tension in your sides. Place the other hand on your hip or thigh for support. For your upper middle back muscles (rhomboid and teres groups) simply hold both arms out in front with hands clenched together, then curl your arms and shoulders forward.

△ Side neck stretch.

△ Rear neck stretch.

◁ Front neck stretch.

△ Upper back stretch.

△ Side stretch.

Lower body stretches

For warming-up purposes, lower body stretches can be kept to an absolute minimum. Choose one basic exercise for each muscle group, namely the groin, thighs, hamstrings and calves.

All these exercises can be performed on the rock or wall to help you combine your flexibility work with an element of climbing technique.

This provides a fun way of breaking up the monotony of an extensive pre-climbing stretching routine.

It is worth consulting an elementary yoga or flexibility training manual for more detailed information. However, it is worth prioritizing the following flexibility exercises, which are especially good for the inner thigh.

THIGH AND QUADRICEPS STRETCH
Stand straight, bending one leg up behind you. Hold your ankle to keep it in position. To increase the stretch, gently push hips forward.

CALF STRETCH
Place both hands against the wall and stretch one leg out straight behind you. Repeat with the other leg.

◁ A good exercise to prepare you for rock-overs or high step-ups.

▷ This exercise stretches the relevant muscles for standing on small holds.

HAMSTRING STRETCH
Sit on the ground, stretching one leg out in front of you, and fold the other leg in. Now gently stretch your upper body forwards.

◁ You can also do this hamstring stretch by standing straight-legged and bending forward to touch the toes. Never bounce, but hold the stretch for 8–12 seconds.

FRONT SPLITS

Although ideal for improving your ability for wide bridging moves, this commonly known exercise requires some care and preferably a few easier groin stretches first to help you work up to it. Simply face front with feet pointing forwards and slowly and carefully ease yourself into a bridge position.

▷ *The leg raise and groin stretch.*

▽ *Front splits and bridge stretch.*

FROG STRETCH

This simple exercise can be performed either standing or lying face down on the floor with your feet slightly wider than shoulder-width apart. Lower your hips towards your feet, turning your knees outwards in a ballet dancer's "plié" position. A great stretch for improving your ability to get your weight close in to the rock.

▷ *The inner thigh frog stretch.*

Progressive build-up

N ow for the really important part. You are warm, mobile and fully stretched, so the final stage is to subject your muscles and tendons to gradually increasing overload (climbing or climbing-related movements of heightened intensity). As mentioned before, use longer sequences to prepare for endurance climbing and shorter programmes to build up for bouldering. Try, also, to make the moves in your warm-up sequences specific to the crag or wall you are about to use. For example, warm up on steep rock if that's what you are mainly going to be doing. Your first movements should be so easy that you barely notice them; use these to relax, stretch out and to tune in mentally to the sensation of climbing. Then, with the use of intermittent rest, build up until you are almost ready for maximum effort. Once you reach this stage, stop and rest for anything between 6–15 minutes

▽ *After you have warmed up and done some light climbing, it is worthwhile to do some more mobility exercises.*

△ *Even outside you can warm up by doing some easy bouldering, before launching yourself on a hard route.*

THE WARM-UP SURVIVAL GUIDE

• Always ensure that all the main three finger grip angles are utilized during the warm-up: crimp, half crimp, and open hand. If necessary try to incorporate slopers, pinches or other more specific types of fingerhold if you know they will be required.

• Ensure that all main arm positions are worked through the full range of motion during the warm-up: pull-down, side-pull, reverse side-pull and undercut.

• Try to climb fluidly, smoothly and in control and only attempt faster dynamic moves to recruit your power and timing towards the end of the warm-up.

• For longer endurance climbing, you will always climb better after incorporating a primary pump into your warm-up to open the capillaries and to activate your body's lactic acid transfer systems.

• The different finger grip angles and arm positions are described on pages 50–55. There is in reality an infinite number, but they break down into specific types of holds.

△ Pinching.

△ Using an undercut hold indoors.

▷ Using an undercut hold on a crag.

before you commence with the climbing session proper. It's worth taking a small amount of fluid and having a light secondary stretch during this period.

PUTTING IT ALL TOGETHER

While this chapter proposes an optimum warming-up model for climbing, it is not intended as a comprehensive guide and should be adapted to suit the requirements of individuals. Above all else, you should warm up in a way that suits your own mental and physical conditioning. Remember that it is always better to make the effort to do something, no matter how simple, for your warm-up and if you're going to set the time aside then you may as well do it properly. After all, the purpose here is to give yourself the best chance of climbing well in addition to avoiding a possible injury.

First steps

Contrary to popular belief, you do not have to be super-muscular with the tenacity of a limpet to be a rock climber. Images in the climbing press do have a tendency to promote this point of view, but there are hundreds of thousands of climbs around the world that require little more than good balance and a head for heights. The first steps on rock can have such a profound influence over subsequent feelings towards this great sport that it is important to take them carefully. A course run by trained and qualified personnel is one of the better ways to be introduced, but many people develop a deep affinity for the sport through friends who are themselves committed climbers. There need be no limitations of age, height or weight for those first steps – whether as a child or pensioner, when you put feet and hands to rock matters little, for there are levels to suit all.

FIRST STEPS

More and more people are introduced to rock climbing through the medium of climbing walls indoors. This is no bad thing, for it does at least allow the beginner to concentrate on

△ Modern instructional techniques allow you to progress to leading easy climbs within a few days of taking your first steps on rock.

◁ An idyllic pose high above a valley. For many climbers, the thrill of an exposed situation spices up the whole experience.

△ Climbing walls are a good medium through which to learn the basics of movement, but try to avoid the steep and strenuous climbs when starting out.

◁ As the rock climb gets steeper you will definitely need muscles and tenacity – and a great deal of experience.

▽ An ideal angle on which to begin. Concentrate on precise footwork and learn to trust the friction properties of your footwear.

movement in a friendly atmosphere that is always warm and dry. Not all climbing walls have suitable facilities for beginners. They are usually too steep and require strength combined with good technique, normally acquired over a period of time. The ideal beginner's venue is a low-angled slab where much of the body weight is taken over the feet rather than relying on arm strength to maintain contact with the rock.

An outdoor crag can be more suitable because of the infinite variety of low-angled rock that can be found. The major disadvantage is, of course, that you cannot guarantee finding warm and dry conditions! Wet rock tends to be very slippery and cold wet rock is certain to put you off forever. Given that ideal conditions are available you should try to find a venue that has a profusion of easy-angled rock with little or nothing in the way of potential danger. Low boulders are ideal, even more so if they have lush grassy ground beneath them or soft sand. Make sure, too, that you are able to descend from the boulder with ease either off the back or by climbing down an easy way. Put on your shoes, and a helmet if there is a chance of loose rock or a fall, and you're away. It is always important to ensure that your feet are dry before you set foot on to the rock. This can be done by wiping the sole on the inside of a trouser leg, with your hand or with a rag specifically carried for this purpose.

Feet and friction

Good footwork is one of the main foundations for good climbing. The skill of precise foot placement enables better balance and movement. Your legs are much stronger than your arms, and the more you learn to use them, the farther and longer you will be able to climb. Most beginners concentrate on where to put their hands, ignoring their feet entirely. This approach should be resisted. You must learn to trust your feet, even on the smallest of holds. The use of rock shoes, with their excellent friction properties, makes this much easier to do.

EASY-ANGLED ROCK
Find a really low-angled piece of rock, say about 25 to 30 degrees, and simply walk around on it. At this angle you will find that it's easily possible to manage without using your hands. Take the opportunity to become acquainted with the superb friction properties of your rock shoes. Try standing on a small ledge of rock with the inside or outside edge of the shoe. Avoid high-stepping movements. Though there are times in rock climbing when you need to make a big step up, a good deal of energy can be saved by utilizing intermediate,

▽ Spend some time before a climb simply walking around on rock without the need for handholds.

△ Economy of effort is essential in rock climbing. Try to avoid high stepping movements when taking those first steps.

perhaps smaller, footholds to reach a more secure one. Keep looking down at your feet and slowly begin to develop precision about where you place them. Each time you put your foot on a hold, it should be placed deliberately and, hardest of all, with confidence that it will stick in place. Try using only the friction between shoe sole and rock to create a foothold. This is known as "smearing".

USING FOOTHOLDS

Having gained some confidence in the stickiness of the shoes, it's time to move on to techniques of standing on specific and obvious holds or ledges. Find a piece of rock that is a little bit steeper and where hands placed against the surface can be used for balance. Balance only, remember! You don't need to use them to pull up on just yet. It was once thought that climbing is more efficient and safer if you maintain three points of contact with the rock at all times, and lean out and away from the rock so that you have a clear view of your feet and the rock in front of you. While this may be useful for easier climbs, in the grand scheme of things it may misdirect you and make later climbing experiences much less efficient.

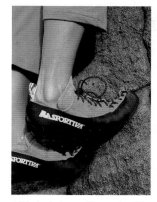

△ The technique of "smearing" the shoes over the rock surface is well illustrated here.

▷ The feet are smeared and the hands are used mainly for balance, though some support may be gained by curling the fingers over the smallest of edges.

● USING SMALL STEPS

It is a good idea to get into the habit of taking small steps up as you climb. This may mean using footholds that are not particularly good. However, it is better to use them and move up for better holds, rather than stretching too high to get to the better holds straight away. Over-reaching immediately puts you off balance and will also put a greater strain on your muscles.

Experiment at your local indoor wall or crag. Choose an easy route (either short, easy bouldering problems or a longer route – but use a rope and be belayed!). Try it first making big reaches with both hands and feet. Now do it again, but taking small steps and making smaller controlled moves. What did you notice?

△ Keep the hands low to avoid over-stretching.

△ Having made the step up, the next handhold is reached.

More footwork

As you gain confidence in your feet, you will come to trust the smaller footholds generally found on harder climbs. Be creative about your approach to footwork, and remember to experiment with your balance, finding out what works and what does not.

▷ *When standing on well-defined ledges, however large or small, try to use the inside of the foot. This will allow you to get your weight closer in to the rock and directly over the foothold.*

▷ *A similar technique is used here, but the outside of one foot is also used to aid upward progress.*

EDGING

Look down towards your feet and try to pick out small or large edges, protrusions and depressions in the rock surface. Each one you find could be a foothold and you should try to use them all, even if it means taking 20 steps to gain a few feet of height. You will quickly discover that by using these features each placement of the foot gains greater security than if it was just smeared on to the hold. If you find an edge that is difficult or uncomfortable to stand on with the front of the shoe, experiment by turning your foot sideways and putting either the inside or the outside edge of the shoe on the hold. This technique will be instantly more comfortable, for the simple reason that you are able to gain more support from the shoe across its width than its length because there is a good deal more rigidity and less leverage

△ *Using the inside and outside of the shoe means you can get more of your foot in contact with the rock, and will ultimately be more comfortable.*

◁ Steeper rock and smaller footholds demand precise footwork and the confidence to stand around while fixing protection or working out the next move.

● CLIMBING BLINDFOLD

At this stage there are lots of little exercises you can do to make learning more fun. One suggestion is to try climbing with a blindfold on and ask a colleague to talk you through the moves. Not only will this help you to gain more awareness of body movement, but the person talking you through the sequence will have to visualize the most efficient sequence for you to follow. Concentrate on being very precise with each foot and handhold. Think about your balance. Being blindfold should help you with this. Be prepared to make lots of small adjustments to your position to find the most efficient body shape to adapt to in the circumstances.

across the sole. When you use the sides of the shoe in this way, it is called "edging". As you venture on to steeper rock, this technique becomes increasingly important.

CROSSING YOUR FEET

Like the often repeated adage regarding three points of contact at all times, ignore those that suggest you should never cross your feet one in front of the other. On a traverse it will be considerably easier if you are able to cross your feet, for it will put you in a good position to transfer body weight over to the next foothold. It is very important that you don't attempt too large a step. Normally your ability to stretch and flex your limbs will dictate the extent to which you can step, so be aware of what your body tells you. If you clearly cannot cope with the stretch, look for alternative and intermediate holds.

△ **1** By crossing one leg inside the other, you are well placed to move comfortably towards the next suitable foothold.

△ **2** The move completed. You are now ready to repeat the sequence and move on to the next holds.

Using handholds

Handholds are more easily seen, generally speaking, than footholds. They are at eye level, or thereabouts. However, they come in all shapes and sizes and at all angles. You will need to experiment to find the best use of them.

JUGS, FINGERHOLDS AND SIDE-PULLS

Having gained some confidence with your feet, it's time to move on to the hands. We have already experimented a little with the hands for balance. Having an edge to curl your fingers over increases the feeling of security, but we are not yet ready to use holds to pull our body weight up the rock – that has to wait for much steeper occasions. To begin, select a section of rock at a 45–50 degree angle and long enough so that you can make several consecutive

moves horizontally or at a slight rising diagonal across the surface. This sideways movement is called "traversing". The benefits of traversing are that you don't need to climb too high above the ground and that you will also get more continuous movement.

Now you need to look not only at your feet and decide where to put them, but also to consider using your hands to make life easier. You will need to use a variety of handholds. The simplest ones to use are those that you pull on from directly below. No doubt these will sometimes feel large and occasionally so small that they might appear inadequate. Large handholds that you can curl all of the fingers of one hand over are usually called "jugs". Climbers, in their early days on rock, also refer to them as "thank God" holds for

▷ *Holds over which you can comfortably curl your hand are sometimes called "thank God" holds. These are the most welcome holds to find on any climb.*

△ *More large handholds, this time inside and along the edges of a diagonal crack. Use your imagination when looking for holds to grip on to.*

It is always a good idea to remove your watch and any rings or other jewellery. Some types of handholds can be very taxing on your fingers and arms, and may cause damage to anything you happen to be wearing. Apart from scratches to your jewellery, you may also suffer damage to yourself if your jewellery becomes trapped. The forces involved could dent a ring into your finger, for example.

◁ *Small fingerholds are surprisingly secure, particularly if there is an incut lip to the edge of the hold.*

◁ *Leaning sideways off a hold will allow you to let go with one hand to reach upward and diagonally. In this case, the climber will be able to let go with the right hand and reach up to better holds above.*

obvious reasons! Holds that you can only get half the length of your fingers on, or your fingertips only, are called "fingerholds".

With these two types of handhold you have enough to be able to climb most moderately graded rock. But other less obvious handholds exist, and to get the best out of them you will need to experiment. For example, a handhold found to lie vertically with the cliff face may at first seem useless. However, if it is pulled on from the side, with your feet positioned to keep you in balance, this type of hold will be found usable. They are called "side-pulls". Side-pulls are great holds to use when traversing, as they help you to pull your body across the rock and to transfer weight from foot to foot. You need to keep a keen eye out for the infinite variety of handholds available. A canny climber will look for, find and use even the most obscure hold to aid progress, so don't dismiss anything lightly.

Planning your moves

The key to climbing efficiently is to be able to read the rock you are about to climb. This will require some imagination (what will it be like to be up there in that position?) and your past experience, and then planning ahead.

CLIMBING MOVES IN SEQUENCE

To climb a section of rock, whether it is a traverse or straight up, you should try to look upon it as a sequence of interlinked movements. To link the movements successfully, you'll need to look beyond the section of rock immediately in front of you and determine where your sequence will end before beginning the next. Sometimes this will be three or four moves and sometimes considerably more. For example, if you have a clear view of a place where you think you can comfortably stand that is about 3 m (10 ft) above, plan a sequence of moves to reach that point.

READING THE ROCK

To successfully plan a sequence of moves, you'll need to look very carefully at the availability of handholds and footholds over the

△ **1** *The objective is clear – first you need to stand up on the right foot and find suitable holds for the hands.*

△ **2** *Pull your weight over on to the right foot and stand up. Keeping as much weight on your right foot as possible …*

△ **3** *… reach up with your right hand for the jug. Here, this sequence of three moves will gain you 1 m (3 ft) in height.*

△ **1** *In this sequence, notice how the feet change position but the left hand stays on the same hold.*

△ **2** *The left hand remains in place to aid balance while an intermediate hold is used by the right hand.*

△ **3** *The left hand changes from a pull hold to a push hold and the feet can be comfortably moved higher, now that there is a secure hold for the right hand.*

section of rock. You will need to think ahead in terms of how you might use the available holds and in what order. An interesting insight into this takes place at indoor climbing competitions. A climber taking part in an indoor climbing competition is allowed to see the route they have to climb a little before they actually have to do it. They will stand at the bottom of the route and scrutinize the holds, trying to visualize where they will be when they get to certain points, how their weight may be distributed, where their hands and feet will be and what technique they might use to move up. They will break the route down into manageable sections. To some extent, all climbers with experience will learn to do this to a certain level to help them cope with the climb they are about to do. Quite often there are many different ways to link holds and moves together in a sequence. These variations depend on what you see, what you think you might be able to use, how far you can

reach and your experience or ability to visualize the moves – often referred to as being able to "read the rock". The way one person climbs a sequence is not necessarily the way that another might link it together, though it is quite right to say that having seen someone climb a piece of rock the next climber to attempt it has a distinct advantage.

● **VERTICAL CHESS**

Some people find it helpful to consider the analogy between climbing and a game of chess. There are an infinite number of moves that you could make but only a few that will lead you into a winning position – and, of course, it is the winning moves that matter most! You might try a bouldering sequence several times, attempting the moves differently each time. Try to gauge which sequence was the most efficient and energy-saving. Try also to analyze what makes a sequence a success or a failure. Climbers often talk about their minds being in tune with what they are trying to do on one day, but out of tune on others. Getting it right is as much a mental achievement as a physical one.

Moving on – a real route

Having spent a few hours practising the basic skills of movement on rock, it is time to move on to something a little more adventurous. The most natural progression is to attempt a short climb on a bottom rope. For advice on how to set up the system, see Chapter 3.

USING A ROPE

When you first climb using a rope, you may feel differently about the whole experience of climbing. There is more to think about than simply making moves. The harness and rope may get in the way, but you will soon get used to them. At this stage try to find a climb that is not too steep, is well endowed with handholds and footholds, and offers a diversity of rock features – by doing so you are assured of success. An ideal height for the climb would be around 10 m (30 ft). Ideals, of course, are rarely

achievable! Before starting out on the climb, stand back and take a good look at the route you think you might take. Look for obvious ledges or breaks in the cliff face, places where you might be able to pause and rest to consider the remainder of the ascent. The knowledge that you gain from this perusal can be used to your advantage in breaking down the climb into short sections that are easier to cope with. You must of course keep the final goal in mind, but don't let it hinder your ability to think calmly.

Remembering the analogy with a game of chess, plan a sequence of moves and put them to the test. If it doesn't quite work out the way you had planned but you still succeed, it matters little. If you find that your calculated sequence doesn't quite work, take a moment to re-think. Do not just look at the rock immediately in front of your nose. Look to the sides of the line you are to take. Quite often there

◁ A short climb, well endowed with holds of all kinds. Here the climber is safeguarded by using a bottom rope safety system.

▷ The same climb being safeguarded with a top rope method. There are advantages and disadvantages to both methods and much will depend on the situation you find yourself in.

△ *Grooves and corners should be straddled for comfort and energy-efficient climbing.*

will be holds off to one side or the other that are not immediately obvious but that you can put a foot or hand on for maintaining balance or resting. They may not be quite the types of big holds you are looking for or expecting to find, but experimentation is quite likely to prove worthwhile.

Grooves and corners in the rock face are usually straddled with both feet and hands for comfort. This is called "bridging" and is a particularly restful and economic way to climb, because much of your body weight is supported by the feet and legs. Find places where you can experiment with taking one hand off, or even both, in order to gain a rest. Climbing on a top rope is totally safe, and though your weight might sag on to the rope, you'll not fall off in the truest sense – it'll only be a slump! Armed with this knowledge, you can forget those worries and concentrate on the task in hand.

Some people find it a useful exercise to climb the same route several times. Each ascent should become more efficient in terms of energy expended and you will learn a great deal about body movement and awareness.

However, rock in all its infinite variety offers so many different combinations of moves that it is as well not to ponder for too long on any particular climb. You need to extend your experience to include widely differing styles of climbing in order to make progress.

△ *An easy-angled slab makes an ideal first climb. Slabs can be surprisingly tiring on the feet and legs, so try to vary the position of your feet frequently.*

◁ *The climbing wall is an ideal place to try things that might be a little too difficult. If you want to attempt something strenuous don't get too demoralized if you find your strength wanes quickly. Your stamina will improve with practice.*

Longer climbs

The next stage is to move on to longer climbs, either single pitch or multi-pitch (see also Chapter 3). Exactly the same principles of movement apply, but bear in mind that you may have to keep energy levels running for longer. It is vitally important to conserve energy and you would do well to

take moments out to deliberately rest during the climb. This means finding a position that is relatively comfortable (by bridging, for example) and allowing yourself time to re-evaluate the situation, to settle yourself into a good frame of mind and to grow accustomed to the situation you find yourself in.

It is in situations like this that your attitude to climbing is important. Your combination of mental and physical resilience will be re-evaluated. A confident approach, tempered with sound judgement and good technique, will stand you in good stead.

COPING WITH EXPOSURE

Many people find sufficient encouragement and motivation to continue from the early steps on low boulders or short single-pitch climbs to attempt longer climbs, but fail to take heed of the fact that longer climbs may have a frightening element that they hadn't bargained for – a big drop below! This is known as "exposure" and it comes in differing degrees and affects individuals in various ways. A small minority of people are so intimidated that they limit themselves ever after to short climbs; but for the majority of others, exposure adds that extra little bit of spice to the outing. Coping with exposure and maintaining concentration on the task of climbing do not always mix well together.

THE FEAR FACTOR

The fear factor has a considerable influence on your ability to climb and the feeling of an airy and forbidding space below your feet tends to

◁ *It is more difficult to find places to rest weary arms on harder climbs, but with imagination and control it is often possible to find something.*

△ Longer, steeper climbs will inevitably require a certain amount of stamina in equal proportion to strength.

▷ The sound of the sea crashing on the rocks below will often add to a feeling of exposure and intimidation.

preoccupy the mind with all kinds of negative thoughts. Mental preparation for this and taking the time to grow with your surroundings are as important as the actual skills of moving over the rock. Unfortunately it is not so easy to practise in a controlled environment, because the fear factor only kicks in when being scared becomes a reality. Everyone who climbs has their own way of overcoming this factor. There are those who seem oblivious to it but they are few in number. Taking time to mentally stand back and consider your position, and to concentrate on the moves that lie ahead, are important ways to overcome the fear factor.

The way forward

Be selective when you choose climbs to undertake. Pay close attention to the grade and the style of the climb. Those route descriptions found in guidebooks that mention things like "an awkward and strenuous chimney" or "make a bold move up the slightly impending arete" or "a thin and worrying sequence leads to a good jug" or "difficult for the short" or "an airy traverse" – are best avoided. They are coded descriptions for things that might be truly scary!

Enlist the company of a sympathetic friend with whom you can share your experiences. You may have encounters that turn out to be monumental and memorable adventures, which can be recounted years and hundreds of thousands of feet of rock later as happy, innocent moments through which a great deal of experience was gained.

▷ *Careful choice of the climbs you undertake will help to boost confidence as you gain experience. Don't attempt anything too difficult too soon.*

△ *A guidebook will help you to find your way but don't expect it to give you a blow-by-blow account of how to climb.*

STARTING TO LEAD

Progress is not normally a hasty affair. However, quite soon after taking your first steps you may want to begin leading your own climbs. Being on the "sharp" end of the rope is a much riskier proposition, so the first climbs you undertake on the lead should be well within your ability. You will need to learn how to place all the protection equipment you carry, how to arrange your own anchor points and stances, and, above all, choose the way ahead based on what you see and the information given in guidebooks. If you begin climbing on a course staffed by qualified personnel, you are likely to be given the opportunity to lead a very short time after starting out. This is no bad thing, for you will quickly learn to appreciate the finer points of climbing and become more attuned to the rock.

Many people take their first leads alongside an instructor who is attached to a fixed rope by means of a mechanical ascending device. The instructor moves up alongside the student

△ Take a long look at the route before setting off and try to work out in advance where the

◁ Differing types of rock require particular techniques and are not always suited to all climbers.

▽ Leading with an instructor alongside provides a valuable learning experience.

and, because they don't need to hold on to the rock at all, is able to stop and talk the student through runner placements, selection of line to climb and even ways to make sequences of moves. It is an invaluable method of learning and one in which progress can be made relatively quickly and painlessly. Of course you may discover that leading is not for you. There are thousands of climbers who have absolutely no desire whatsoever to lead, but still get great rewards from rock climbing.

Though there are superstars who shine through within a few years of starting out, for many the road is slower. This has advantages in that by the time you are climbing difficult rock the experience amassed stands you in good stead where safety is concerned. However you begin and however long you

climb, savour those first innocent steps into the vertical world – they are but a tantalizing morsel of the riches beyond.

Defining your terms

Thumb sprags, slopers, crimps and smears are all climbing holds and key words of the rock climber's world. But to the uninitiated they are probably meaningless – this chapter should bring enlightenment! In previous pages we have already mentioned a few holds that are commonly used and simple techniques to employ them to best effect. As you gain more experience, you'll discover that a broader repertoire of holds is required. What follows is a brief look at these types of holds, and where and how they can be used most effectively.

JUG, BUCKET OR "THANK GOD" HOLD

These are huge holds that you can curl all your hand over, rather like holding on to the rungs of a ladder (see also page 40). Jugs instill great confidence for the simple reason that you can hang off them without strength draining away too quickly. Any jug that appears at the end of a particularly harrowing sequence of moves is always very welcome, hence its more descriptive term of "thank God" hold. Large holds are often a good place to linger, taking a well-earned rest (or semi-rest). You can also look ahead to see what's in store.

▷ *The ultimate "thank God" hold. The only worry is whether or not it will bear the full weight of the climber!*

FINGERHOLDS

These are small versions of jugs. The finest fingerhold to use is one that has a small lip to it or is incut at the back. Though you might only be able to curl the ends of your fingers over the edge, it is generally sufficient for a fairly strong pull. Fingerholds are sometimes flat and are fine to pull on from directly below but much harder to hang on to if they are at shoulder level. Normally you'd use a flat fingerhold with fingers bent 90 degrees at the main joint. If, however, you can only get the very tips of your fingers on the hold, you must arch the main joint above the hold and keep the fingers rigid. It helps to place your thumb over the first finger as well so that it can take some of the load. This is sometimes referred to as a "crimp". You might also find some relief from levering your thumb against a protrusion or edge if it's available. By levering inwards or pushing outwards, it makes the fingers feel more securely gripped to the rock.

▽ A tiny ledge can be crimped (as held by the lower hand) or held with the tips of the fingers.

△ A flat edge can be gripped with at least half the length of the fingers to provide a secure hold.

△ An incut fingerhold, though small, usually feels very positive.

Creative handholds

As we found out on pages 40–41, handholds are not always what they seem. Sometimes, to get the most out of them, you need to be a little creative in your use of them. Here are a few more tips on how to use marginal holds or to create a hold where there doesn't appear to be one!

SLOPER OR ROUNDED HOLD

These types of hold do not generally instill confidence and are particularly worrying the smaller they become. A sloper that you can get your whole hand over can be made to feel fairly secure provided that you can keep your whole arm and body weight directly below it. Basically, what you do is to try to smear the whole hand over the rock and rely on friction and pressure to hold the hand in place.

Sometimes you can slot fingers into tiny depressions in the rock to give valuable extra purchase. Slopers, though they are found on most types of rock, are more prevalent on sandstone and gritstone, and granite that has been worn by water. The classic, if not particularly encouraging, place to come across slopers is at the top of a gritstone crag. Often you can achieve extra pulling power and grip by smearing part of your arm over the rock as well.

PALMING

This is exactly what it says it is – pushing on the inside of the palm. It can be implemented in several ways, each of which is applicable to different types of move. One of the ways it is most usefully employed is where you have a good positive handhold for one hand and need

◁ Sloping handholds may not provide much confidence but you must make the most of what is available.

▷ Imaginative use of a "palming" technique allows the climber to make a high step.

to make a clean, big step up on to a good foothold. Pulling up on the jug with one hand and pushing down on the rock with the palm of the other lightens the weight on each arm, pushes you further away from the cliff face and allows you to make a high step up. Another application for palming is in climbing corners or grooves where there are few handholds. By pressurizing each palm on either side of the corner or groove, you can relieve enough weight from one foot at a time in order to move them higher. There are climbs where this technique, along with smearing for the feet, are the only techniques that will get you up the climb. Needless to say, climbing long sections of rock devoid of any other types of handholds and footholds can be a harrowing experience.

UNDERCLING

Undercling holds are used in many different ways and, when used imaginatively, prove to be one of the most versatile of all for resting between sequences of moves. The most frequently found use for the undercling is in situations where you are confronted with having to make a move over an overlap or

△ An undercut hold is less tiring on the arms when resting.

▷ Undercut holds will also allow you to lean out and look up the rock to see where you are going.

▽ Relying wholly on friction for both feet and for both hands requires confidence in the friction properties between boot and rock, and skin and rock.

overhang. These features on a rock face often have a crack running horizontally beneath which the hands can be slotted in, with the palms facing upwards. Pulling outwards on your arms allows you to arch your back out and pop your head over the obstacle to see what lies ahead. Once you have found suitable handholds over the lip, you can move one hand over while keeping the other firmly gripped in the undercling. Having taken a good grip of the hold over the lip, release the undercling and move the hand up to another hold and pull yourself around or over the overhang. You can use underclings in many other situations. Basically, any hold that you can get your fingers or your whole hand into from underneath is an undercling. Even if there isn't a hole or crack, a small edge might suffice. On steeper rock underclings are used to best advantage to help you rest and recover enough for the next sequence of moves.

More creative handholds

The weakest link in your body climbing machine is in the fingers. Once you have progressed on to steeper, harder climbs, this will become apparent. To use the types of holds described here, you will need to build up your finger strength.

PINCH-GRIP

Whenever you use a hold between fingers and thumb it's called a pinch-grip. They come in many shapes and sizes, from small and rounded to large and square, and can be used sideways, lengthways or on a diagonal. One of the typical features of limestone rock is the tufa, which is a calciferous flow that hardens over time and usually stands proud of the rock surface. Tufa is the ultimate pinch-grip hold as there are quite often little indents into which you can place your fingers for extra grip. You can also pinch sharp edges of rock in a fairly open-handed grip and gain some security for an upward, or sideways pull. Small knobbles

of rock that protrude from the surface are another type of pinch-grip. A good way to train for increasing the power of your pinch-grip is to lift concrete building blocks – it also toughens the ends of your fingers!

POCKETS

Pockets or holes in the rock are most commonly found on limestone crags, but they are by no means exclusive to limestone. They vary in size tremendously from holes that you can only insert one or two fingers into, to great big ones that you can get both hands in at the same time. They are frequently deep enough to get most of the length of the fingers into, and so even though they might be small they offer excellent grip if you have the finger strength to hang on and pull up. Pockets sometimes have a lip on the upper inside and, having used one to pull up on, you may then be able to turn it into an undercling hold when you move above it.

△ An open-handed pinch-grip is useful for maintaining balance.

△ A finger pocket combined with a pinch-grip by the thumb.

△ A one-finger pocket requires strong fingers.

△ *Here, the weight is taken mainly over the left foot with layaway handholds to maintain the climber's position.*

▷ *The left hand has an open-hand pinch-grip held in an undercut position, while the right hand holds an inverted side-pull or layaway.*

SIDE-PULLS OR LAYAWAYS

Side-pulls are commonly used to allow you to lean sideways to reach another hold that would otherwise be difficult to get to. They are also used to pull yourself sideways on to a foothold that is off to one side or the other. The sides of cracks, regardless of size, can be used to pull sideways on, or to layaway off, and so also can any edges that run vertically on the rock surface. They can also be used to gain a rest, provided the rest of the body is in balance. Simply lean away from the hold and try to keep your arm straight. An arm that is straight rests on the bones and joints, and saves the muscles from becoming more fatigued in the process.

Unusual positions

There are usually several ways in which to overcome an obstacle. However, some of these ways will be more efficient in terms of energy expended than others. This is where good technique comes in to play. Here are a few special techniques to try out, experiment with and then make part of your everyday climbing repertoire.

LAYBACKING

Laybacking is a technique that requires the hands and feet to work in unison. The handholds you use are layaways or side-pulls and feet are usually smeared or placed on any available edges. It is a powerful series of moves in which the hands pull in one direction and the feet push in another. Such is the force generated that in a full-on layback if your hands lose their grip you'll almost certainly catapult out and away from the rock! As a series of linked moves, laybacking is very strenuous indeed and it is sometimes very difficult to take one hand off to place or remove protection. When you do take one hand off, the balance of power between feet and hands is altered and there is a tendency to swing outwards towards the direction of your feet. This rather unnerving phenomenon is known by climbers as "barn-dooring". Layback techniques can also be used as an isolated move to gain holds higher up either on the side of a crack or on small edges in the rock surface.

△ **1** *The layback position uses opposing forces from feet and hands.*

△ **2** *As your feet get closer to your hands, the forces increase.*

△ **3** *Maintain pressure on the feet and one hand, and move the other hand up.*

△ **4** *Now move your feet up again towards your hands …*

△ **5** *… and keep going for as long as you need to.*

MANTLESHELFING

This is a technique rather than a hold, as such. The simplest scenario is one in which you have a ledge to get on to but there are no holds above the ledge that you can reach or use. It requires considerable effort on steep ground, where you might find it difficult to use your feet to help you. You have to reach up to the edge of the ledge and take hold of it with both hands, about shoulder width apart. You then give an almighty heave to bring your shoulders level with the ledge. If you are able, you should try to run your feet up the rock using the smearing technique. Using the momentum you have initiated, keep going upwards until you can turn one hand around into a palming pressure hold on the ledge and lock the arm by bending it at the elbow and throwing your head and shoulders over the top of it. You need to hold that position momentarily while you get the other arm into a similar position, and from there you straighten your arms with another heave and at the same time bring one foot up on to the ledge just on the outside of one arm. Transfer your weight immediately on to this foot and push up on your leg with all your might. As the leg straightens you can bring the other foot up on to the ledge and, in one dynamic movement, stand up.

That is the theory; the practice is considerably different and in the majority of instances you'll end up throwing yourself on to the ledge with a belly roll and then, accompanied by a great deal of leg kicking, nudge the rest of your body on until you are lying sideways on the ledge. Not as graceful but almost as effective!

△ **1** *Get a good grip of the ledge and walk your feet up as high as possible.*

△ **2** *Change the hand grip to a push down and straighten the arms.*

△ **3** *Move one foot up on the ledge by the side of your hands.*

◁ **4** *It is important to keep the arms as straight as is feasibly possible.*

▷ **5** *Finally bring up the second foot and stand up. Mantleshelfing requires a good deal of flexibility in the legs and body.*

Chimneying

This is a technique that you will either love or hate! Chimneys are large fissures in a rock face that will accommodate an entire climber. They can be so tight that there is very little room to manoeuvre, just wide enough to have your back on one side and feet on the other, or so broad that you have to straddle across them with arms and legs spread wide. The techniques for differing widths vary slightly. The classic technique is called back-and-footing. The clearest way to interpret this technique is that you push your back against one wall of the chimney while your feet push against the other and you use these opposing forces to hold you in position.

You don't even need to have handholds and footholds; pressure is sufficient. Although it's easy to hold yourself in, moving up can feel insecure if you take the pressure off. The correct technique for upward progress is vital. Place the palms of both hands on either side of you and just above buttock level. Pressurize them, push your back slightly away from the wall and move up until your buttocks are just above your hands, then immediately lean on to your back. Keeping your palms against the rock, you can then move your feet up, one at a time, until they are on the same level as your bottom. Repeat this process until you reach the end of the chimney. It is helpful if your legs

△ A classic back-and-foot position.

△ The technique of upward progress alternates between these two body positions (left and above).

△ In narrower chimneys it may be possible to utilize the knee for extra security.

◁ *A tight chimney will be awkward but will feel very secure. Note the pressure or palming handhold used to wedge the body more tightly and to help push upwards.*

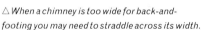

△ *When a chimney is too wide for back-and-footing you may need to straddle across its width.*

◁ *By squirming with the body and pushing with all your might on feet and hands, it is possible to move upwards.*

don't have to be stretched fully out; a little bend at the knees helps you to exert greater pressure. Make sure that you take only short movements each time in order to maintain the security of the wedge and, if you can, use footholds and handholds to advantage.

Tight chimneys that allow little room for movement are climbed using similar principles but upward progress is achieved more by a wriggling technique in combination with pressure on either side of the chimney. When a chimney is so wide that back-and-footing is impossible, you will need to straddle the gap. Handholds and footholds are more crucial to success, as it is often quite difficult to get a high degree of opposing pressure to keep you in place. By their very nature, chimneys are fairly dark and dingy places and it can be extremely difficult to actually see the rock features in order to find holds – allow your eyes time to accustom to the poor light.

Jamming

amming is a technique used in smooth-sided, virtually holdless cracks. If you are adept at using them and a suitable crack exists, you might also jam as an alternative to using normal handholds. The technique is exactly as the term "jamming" suggests;

what it doesn't tell you, though, is how painful it can be if executed incorrectly, damaging the hand in the process.

HAND JAMS

A crack that is suitable for a hand jam is called a "hand crack". Clearly, what might be a hand crack for a person with small hands is likely to be a tight hand crack for someone larger. Assuming that you can get your hand into the crack, place it open-handed. Find a spot where there is about 1–2 cm (½–¾ in) clearance either side of the hand then push the thumb

◁ ▽ *A nearly perfect hand crack will provide very secure jams. On first acquaintance jamming may seem painful, but as you gain more experience a good jam becomes something of a "thank God" type of hold.*

into the palm of the hand. As you do, arch your hand across the crack so that the fingers are pushing against one side and the back of your hand against the other. It is important to stretch the skin as tightly as you can across the back of the hand, as this will prevent the skin from getting too badly damaged. Once you feel the tightening action happen, continue to arch your hand as much as possible. This will tighten the jam and make it much more secure – though it will be difficult to believe it at first! Now you can put some weight on it and see if it works.

FIST JAMS

When a crack is too large for a hand jam, it may be possible to jam your fist into it. The basic theory is very similar in that you need to keep the skin taut across your hand, and you must keep the pressure on as long as you need the jam to grip. There are two ways to jam the fist. One is quite simply to make a fist and the other is with the thumb pressed inside curled fingers.

Fist jams can be used effectively in parallel-sided cracks or in tapered cracks. Normally you would use them with the back of the hand

△ A well-placed hand jam – push the thumb into the palm and arch your hand across the crack to create a sound hold.

△ When a crack is too wide for a hand jam, try wedging the fist into the crack. Make sure that the thumb is tucked inside the palm.

facing out from the crack but in a great many situations you will find them more comfortable to use if the inside of the hand faces outwards. One hand each way is a useful technique to employ for repeated fist-jamming movements.

● FOOT JAMS

Any part of the body can be used to jam with. The toes, or better still, the whole foot, can be utilized in a suitable-sized crack. Toes can be jammed into narrow cracks, about the size you would use for your fingers or hands. The whole foot can be used, either straight in, or placed sideways if the crack is large enough. You must be careful, however, not to jam your foot too deeply into a crack. It is remarkably easy to get a foot well and truly wedged in. This will make moving up impossible! Try to achieve a jam that gives enough security to use successfully, but will not prove a hindrance when moving on.

▷ This shows a foot jam wedged sideways across a wide crack.

Finding rests on a route

The ability to find resting positions while in the most unlikely climbing situations pays enormous dividends. On easier climbs there are frequently large ledges to accommodate the whole foot, the rock angle lays back and all the weight can be taken over the feet. On steeper ground it may not be possible to stand in a position where you can take both hands off to rest. You might find yourself standing on a tiny foothold with the edge of one shoe and very little for the other foot. Handholds might be smaller than you would like and the aura of the situation might be very intimidating. By using your imagination, it is usually possible to find a rest of sorts.

KEEPING CLOSE INTO THE ROCK

On steep rock you must keep your body pushed up against the rock surface and the body weight directly over the feet. To achieve this a fine positioning of the body may be required and the difference of a few centimetres one way or the other can often make a significant difference. To stand efficiently on tiny toeholds, you'll need to use the inside edge of your rock shoe. The reasons for this are simple enough – you need to glean as much support as you can from the shoe and the lateral rigidity offers more than the longitudinal rigidity. It is also possible to stand on the outside edge of the shoe but it is less effective for upward movement unless you are making moves across the rock face. As an aid to resting, however, you'll find it very useful for relieving pressure and tension from cramped feet.

RESTING YOUR ARMS

Try not to hang on too tightly with the hands and arms. Concentrate wholly on placing as much weight as possible over the feet and if your feet tire change position occasionally. The ideal resting handhold is a side-pull or under-cut. The reasons for this are simple enough – the arm is in a fairly low position where blood can flow freely to the muscles. If you are hanging on to a hold above your head, the blood will drain from your arms and the muscles will not be replenished with oxygen.

◁ *Resting between difficult sections of a climb is vitally important and every opportunity should be taken.*

△ By varying the holds that you use, arms and fingers are less likely to cramp up.

△ Arms can be rested most effectively by dangling them at full stretch to allow the blood to flow back into the fingers. Alternate arms for effective rests.

If you are forced to hang on holds above your head, you must try to rest each arm by alternately dangling each down below waist level and shaking the hand loosely to assist blood flow. This is called "shaking out". Try not to rush the process. If you are very tired, it takes a good 5 minutes or more to rest adequately and recover sufficient energy to continue. By moving on before you are properly rested, you'll find that strength wanes very rapidly to the extent that you might not have enough power to complete a sequence. If you have to, don't be afraid to back down to a "no-hands" resting-place, even though it might mean down-climbing a fair distance. It is all about maximizing the remaining power to achieve the next rest or the end of the difficulties.

◁ Sometimes a full rest can be found by climbing down a few feet to a ledge. This is the best possible rest you can have.

Saving your arms

Rests where you are able to use under-cut holds or side-pulls are generally more efficient. You only use strength to hold body weight in to the rock surface rather than hang on. Of course, holds such as these are not always available and some imagination may be required to find the most effective resting position. If you have to hang on to large holds above your head, it's worth trying to open up the hand as much as possible. Big jugs or flat holds can be held with the palm where the wrist is bent over at 90 degrees like a hook – rest with a straight arm to save the precious energy in your muscles. Again, try to alternate hands so that you get a good rest for each arm.

△ A combination of heel-hook with the foot wedged in the crack adds security while also being effective for saving strength.

△ A large jug or ledge can be held in a hook grip for greater comfort.

◁ Experiment with different body positions to find the most comfortable rest.

Crack climbing can be extraordinarily trying and tiring. Feet and hands become cramped from continually being wedged into the crack. If the crack is wide enough, it might be possible to get a hands-off rest by wedging your knee into the crack and levering your foot against one side. This is called a knee-bar. Knee-bars may also be found anywhere where there is a suitable feature and can sometimes even be effected on open features such as below overlaps or overhangs.

The heel-hook is another good way to save energy and it is used to surmount overhangs. It is exactly what it sounds like – by hanging underneath an overhang by your hands, the foot is brought up to the same level and hooked on to a suitable protrusion or ledge. You can take a surprisingly large proportion of the strain from your arms by using the foot and the leg as a lever. The drawback with this is that you do need to be rather gymnastic and flexible, for it is a powerful manoeuvre.

In a similar vein is the toe-hook. Whilst not used as a powerful movement, it is a useful way to maintain balance or equilibrium. Take one example – on a layback sequence you find it difficult to prevent the opposing forces, of feet pushing while hands pull, causing you to swing outwards. This rather alarming effect is known as "barn-dooring" and once it comes into effect it is a struggle to prevent the inevitable flying fall. If you can hook the toe of one boot into a crack or behind a rib of rock, it is possible to use it to hold your body stable while you try to move into a position of more security. Toe-hooks can sometimes be used to help gain a rest in an otherwise seemingly impossible situation.

▷ *A toe-hook in a large hole provides leverage for the move up as well as helping to gain a useful rest.*

▽ *The arms will not tire so quickly if they are used at full stretch or fully bent.*

Energy-saving techniques

By far the most efficient and energy-saving way to climb is to use the technique of bridging. This was, of course, a technique that we introduced right at the very beginning when we took our first steps on rock and it is something that we can apply, with some imagination, to many situations encountered on more difficult climbs. It is possible, for example, to use a bridging technique on a steep, open wall where none of the more recognizable features of grooves and corners are apparent. You might find yourself taking all your weight on the very tip of the inside of the toe of your shoe. This is an incredibly tiring position for the foot to be in for any protracted period of time, but if you are able to reach out and push sideways with the other foot it is possible to alleviate much of the strain.

An "Egyptian" or "drop knee" is a useful technique to conserve energy on very steep rock. It is a comfortable position that allows you to keep the torso very close in to the rock surface and more weight on the feet and legs than would normally be possible. As the illustration (right) shows, however, it is an advantage to be able to contort the body and to retain flexibility. It is such an unconventional technique to employ that many climbers forget its usefulness. Milder forms and shapes than that shown can be achieved in a great many climbing scenarios – all it requires is some imagination.

MORE DYNOS!

Dyno is a shortened term for dynamic motion. A dyno move is one in which the climber utilizes momentum to their advantage. Take

◁ Any feature that can be straddled by bridging across it is likely to be less tiring.

▷ The same feature climbed using the technique of back-and-footing, which is most commonly associated with chimney climbing.

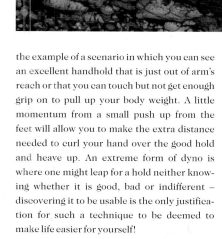

△ On steep, open climbs it is often difficult to engineer a rest position. You will be reliant on good footwork and stamina to get you through.

◁ Here the toe is hooked to a hold to help secure the body in close, thus permitting weight to be borne by the foot and directly below the handgrips. This is sometimes called an Egyptian or "drop knee".

the example of a scenario in which you can see an excellent handhold that is just out of arm's reach or that you can touch but not get enough grip on to pull up your body weight. A little momentum from a small push up from the feet will allow you to make the extra distance needed to curl your hand over the good hold and heave up. An extreme form of dyno is where one might leap for a hold neither knowing whether it is good, bad or indifferent – discovering it to be usable is the only justification for such a technique to be deemed to make life easier for yourself!

"Flagging" is a term applied to describe a technique that is a perfectly natural movement of the body in motion, retaining balance. It is simple enough to use in a huge number of climbing scenarios at any grade – except perhaps the easiest, where it may be frowned upon as unnecessary and energy-wasting. It is often interpreted as a thrashing or leg-kicking movement – the fact that it is useful seems to be overlooked. The leg is used in one of two ways in flagging, either as a counterbalance to maintain equilibrium or as a pendulum action to assist in dynamic motion.

More energy-saving tips

There are other things not directly associated with body movement or holds that will help you conserve energy on steeper climbs. These include the efficiency with which you are able to place protection on the lead and also how you carry or "rack" your gear. There are several ways in which you can do this and every climber will, over time, learn which is the most suitable for their preferences. This does require experimentation and a mind open to change.

Considerable energy can be wasted trying to fiddle a nut into a crack that it clearly will not fit. Sometimes you look at a crack and be so convinced that a particular-sized nut will fit in that you become blind to other possibilities,

▷ *Whenever you place runners on steep rock, try to find good holds and a comfortable position from which to operate.*

whether of size of nut or even a different part of the crack! You will gain considerable advantage if you carry nuts of a similar size on individual karabiners, say large on one, medium on another and small on a third. If one nut doesn't fit the crack, there will almost certainly be another on the karabiner that will.

PREPARING PROTECTION

Many climbers, when faced with a difficult or crucial nut placement, will prepare themselves while in a comfortable position. If you know, or are fairly positive, that one particular-sized nut is likely to fit into the crack, you could remove it from the rack and if necessary clip in a quickdraw, and then move up to the placement with it held in your teeth. Once you reach the right spot all you need to do is to place it! Obviously you must be certain of the size, because if you're not you will needlessly waste valuable energy.

Some harness manufacturers have developed a special plastic clip for connecting a karabiner to; using the karabiner becomes simply a matter of pulling it rather than unclipping from the gear loop. It is helpful to rack gear in a particular order that you become familiar with. This, too, will save precious energy. Quickdraws, any nuts on rope slings and camming devices also need to be carefully positioned so that they are accessible almost by feel alone. Many items of protection equipment are colour-coded by the manufacturer – long winter evenings can be whiled away learning all the codes for your personal rack. No single method can be said to be categorically the best, so it is important to experiment and adapt a method to suit your needs. You may even find that you come to favour particular pieces of protection. Keep them to hand.

△ **1** *A runner gripped between the teeth ready for placement will save valuable energy on steep rock.*

△ *When you rack your gear, make sure you work with a system that you are happy and familiar with.*

▽ *The climber checks out the way ahead. In doing this, he may save precious energy once on the climb.*

△ **2** *You just have to hope it's the right size!*

Clipping the rope

Efficient clipping of the rope has two main benefits: you save energy the quicker you can perform the task, and there are ways to clip that increase your safety in the event of a fall.

The method by which you clip the rope into protection can also make a tremendous difference to the energy you expend. It is difficult to comprehend perhaps, but a fumbled clip could conceivably lead to dire consequences such as a long fall on the sharp end of the rope.

There are any number of ways to clip the rope into a runner efficiently. Like racking, it is as well to experiment with several before latching on to a method that suits your preferences and dexterity. Regardless of the method adopted, there are two important aspects to remember. Firstly, the gate of the karabiner

◁ *On sustained and steep climbs, energy conservation is crucial to success.*

▽ *Practise clipping the rope into running belays until you can do it blindfold!*

△ A quickdraw clipped correctly with the straight-gate karabiner clipped to the bolt, and the rope running through the bent-gate karabiner.

In this situation, the bent-gate karabiner has been clipped to the bolt. This will make it harder to clip the rope. The quickdraw should basically be the other way round (see far left).

◁ It is not so easy to clip the rope into a straight-gate karabiner.

into which you are clipping the rope should face away from the immediate direction you are going to be climbing in. This is to ensure that, in the event of a fall, the rope does not unclip itself. Secondly, you must ensure that the quickdraw is not twisted in any way once the rope is clipped in. A twist in the sling of the quickdraw can in rare cases also allow the rope to become unclipped in the event of a fall. It is a simple enough matter of adopting good habits in ensuring both aspects are observed.

One suggested method of clipping the rope into a quickdraw is illustrated. If you are clipping the rope into a runner that is way above your head you might have to pull a short length of rope up, grip it in your teeth and then pull up more so that you have enough slack rope to reach up and make the clip. Once the rope is in the karabiner, you can release the teeth grip and continue climbing. Holding the rope momentarily in the teeth means that you don't have to heave with all your might on the rope to pull it up to make the clip, and thus saves valuable energy resources. If, for whatever reason, you think you might fall off while you are

attempting the clip, don't forget to drop the rope from your teeth as you fall – only circus performers can hold someone in their teeth on the end of a trapeze!

◁ A well-placed nut, with the quickdraw clipped to it.

Falling off

Though falling is something that every climber must come to terms with, there are those to whom the idea is complete anathema and there are others to whom it is par for the course. To achieve the utmost purity of style, you should always try to climb without falling. This is called an "on-sight" ascent. Not so many years ago there was a saying amongst climbers that the "leader never falls". In times past this was a good adage to work to because there was little, if any, protection on a pitch. Today the situation has changed significantly. Leading climbs has become less of a risky business as equipment for arranging crack protection has developed and improved. There are still climbs on which it is impossible to arrange adequate protection, but they are fewer in number.

MODERN ATTITUDES

Purity of style and ambition to climb hard are not always good bed partners. Ambition can become headstrong and ignore purity entirely. More commonly, ambition will bring purity around to its way of thinking and a compromise is reached that is acceptable to both. Many climbers will push themselves beyond their "on-sight" grade, knowing full well that they will probably fall off at the crux and may do so several times before successfully completing the sequence. This ethic or compromise approach is better conducted on bolted or "sport" climbs where you know full well that the runners on to which you are falling will be capable of absorbing the shock of repeated falls. Traditional routes, where one places one's own protection, are not always so

△ The old adage, "the leader never falls", was sound advice in the days when climbers tied the rope directly around their waists.

▷ While the modern-day climber with all the safety trappings is more secure, it is still purer to climb without falling. You may find an acute lack of protection on some climbs!

◁ A steep bolt-protected climb is an ideal place to practise falling off!

▷ Make sure that you push yourself clear of the rock and look down to see where you're heading to.

reliable. It is an accepted method of climbing, but it may not be entirely satisfactory to all climbers. Knowing that it is relatively safe to fall off helps you to keep your composure. At the extreme end of the scale there are climbs of high technical difficulty where the prospect of falling will mean certain death – if you attain those levels one would assume that you have advanced far beyond the scope of this book.

FALLING TECHNIQUE

Taking a fall will come to most leaders at some time. This may be on to bolts at the wall or on a sport climb, or it may be on to gear that the leader has placed. It is important to understand that it is not the act of falling that puts the climber in danger of injury – it is the impact with the rock face, wall, ledge or even the ground itself. Falling into space may be frightening, but provided that is all it is there should be no problem. It will be evident from this that, provided the protection is good and holds, falling off overhanging hard climbs is safer than falling off an easy slab. Falling off a slab means that the climber will come into contact with rock. There some tips for falling more safely. For example, you can push your-

◁ It is easier to attempt climbs that are beyond your current ability on an indoor wall – here falling off is much less serious.

self away from the wall or rock, rather than clinging on and scraping down the surface, doing untold damage. However, this takes a lot of experience and courage to do. The natural instinct is to cling!

Tips for seconding

When discussing techniques and ways to conserve energy, it is easy to forget that seconding a climb can sometimes be as tiring as leading. It may not be as mentally stressful (the fear factor should not be as great as that involved in lead-ing a climb), but stress levels could easily be equal in terms of frustration. Climbing tech-niques apply in the same way, but when it comes to taking out protection, energy loss can be outrageously high.

MENTAL ATTITUDE

Seconding a climb, if you are more used to leading, is generally approached in a rather lackadaisical manner and with the attitude that it'll be a lot easier on the blunt end of the rope. Climbers who set off to follow a pitch in this frame of mind will quite commonly get caught out and surprised by the awkwardness of the climbing. If at the same time they expe-rience difficulties removing runners that the leader has placed, the whole experience could prove quite harrowing.

REMOVING RUNNERS

Sometimes, particularly on the crux of a climb or on sections where it is preferable to keep going, the second might well decide to remove the runners from the crack but leave them on the rope rather than waste valuable energy unclipping them and clipping them on to the harness. When you arrive at a more comfort-able place to rest, the runners can be removed from the rope and placed on the harness. If a piece of protection proves difficult to remove and it is clear that you are going to waste a lot of strength getting it out, it may be better to ask the leader for a tight rope to take your full body weight while you fiddle the offending piece out. It is always a good excuse for a rest!

◁ On serious climbs of great difficulty the role of the second is vital. Having confidence in the second allows the leader to concentrate on the all-absorbing task of leading.

△ Sometimes you'll find it more difficult to second climbs than you would if you were leading – it's an odd fact of life!

▷ Traverses, particularly difficult ones, can be intimidating and very serious for the second.

● TRAVERSING AND DOWN-CLIMBING

There are certain situations in which seconding a climb can be as risky as leading it. An unprotected traverse is one such situation. Here, if a seconding climber comes off, he or she will swing down and out. If this happens on one of the numerous sea-cliff traverses that can be found around the world, the situation could be particularly exciting! A knowledge of prussiking will come in useful (see Chapter 3).

Another tricky situation for the second involves down-climbing. If the moves are not protected from above, a fall could be a long one. In these situations, the second needs to be as confident and capable as the leader.

ROPEWORK

Ropework is a fundamental part of modern rock climbing. It is worth practising the techniques described until they become second nature. There are usually several ways of doing things, but the methods shown here are simple and quick to learn. Ropework can be daunting, but taking things one step at a time will help. Do not try to remember everything at once. When learning new skills, it is important to remember the principles behind the instruction. By doing this, it should be easier to remember the steps as progress is made. This step-by-step approach to the ropework required for climbing should provide the tool kit needed to cope with most situations. It is up to the climber to dip into that tool kit and find the necessary tools required.

Opposite: *An exposed, hard route. Although the climbing is relatively straightforward, good judgement, a thorough knowledge of modern ropework and a cool head are necessary for a safe ascent.*

Fitting the harness

Many different designs of harness are available. Most are manufactured in one piece – the leg loops are an integral part of the harness. Some harnesses are "one size fits all", while others are produced in small, medium and large sizes. Some have adjustable leg loops which allow you to wear the harness over several layers of clothing if needed. Those harnesses without adjustable leg loops will require a little more judgement to ensure a good fit.

DOING THE HARNESS UP

Almost all harnesses rely on a double-back system on the buckle. The waistbelt has to be threaded though both parts of the buckle and back through one. This will hide half the buckle and form a "C" for closed and not "O" for open. If the buckle is not doubled back, it can come undone. There are several harness manufactures using different designs, so it must be stressed that in all cases the manufacturer's instructions must be followed to the letter.

△ This is a simple harness designed specifically for beginners. The waist belt cannot be undone completely so a "step-in" system is used. There is minimal provision for equipment-carrying, which makes this this harness more suitable for indoor venues.

◁ Here a climber is being lowered off a modern sport route. The consequences of an uncomfortable or incorrectly fastened harness need only be imagined.

Leg loops may be padded, to a greater or lesser extent, on the inside for comfort. Leg loop buckles should be doubled back like the waist belt, and should be on the outside of the leg. When putting a harness on, ensure the waist belt goes around the waist and not over the hips, and that the leg loops are positioned comfortably at the top of the leg and base of the buttocks.

If the harness has adjustable leg loops, adjust the waist belt part of the harness first and then the leg loops. This should ensure the correct fit. If the leg loops are tightened first, there will be a tendency not to position the waist belt correctly, leaving it too low on the hips. This is particularly important on harnesses that are designed to be put on without having to step into the leg loops, often referred to as a "nappy system" harness.

△ The buckle system is vitally important. Here the strap has not been doubled back, making the harness extremely dangerous because only a small amount of force will be necessary to release the buckle.

△ Here the "C" for closed is clearly visible and although not all harnesses employ the same fastening system, most are very similar. Take the time to look for an obvious way of checking your own and other people's harnesses easily.

● GETTING IT WRONG

There are a number of problems that may occur fitting a harness. The main ones are:

① Not getting the right position around the waist
② Not doing the buckle correctly
③ Getting a twist in the harness or leg loop

There have been many instances where expensive harnesses have been put on incorrectly in the enthusiasm to get on with the climb, but it must be stressed a little care and attention to detail is important at this stage. Spend a couple of minutes doing this job correctly. It is vitally important! Before you climb, make one last check.

△ The leg loops are too tight and the harness is positioned over the hips, making the centre of gravity too low. In the event of a slip, the climber could turn upside down.

△ This picture illustrates how easy it is to see an incorrectly fastened harness when clothing is tucked into the harness – however much or little clothing you happen to be wearing.

△ This is a comedy of errors! The support straps for the leg loops are crossed and the right leg loop is twisted, putting unnecessary strain on the stitching.

Attaching the rope

Although there are many different designs of harness on the market, the method of tying the rope shown here is almost universal. The rope loop formed around the harness is not only important for the climber but forms an essential part of rope work outdoors, so it is important to get this right from the start.

TYING THE FIGURE-OF-EIGHT KNOT
It is vitally important to do this correctly. The harness and rope are both incredibly strong, but both are useless if they are not joined correctly. Most people use what is called a figure-of-eight knot, although some climbers prefer the bowline. Harnesses will have slight variations on where the rope is threaded and you must refer to the manufacturer's instructions and follow them implicitly.

△ **1** To tie a figure-of-eight knot, form a loop of rope a little over 1 m (3 ft) from the end of the rope.

△ **2** Now twist the loop and pick up the end of the rope. Push this through the loop to form a figure-of-eight knot in the rope.

△ **3** The end of the rope goes through the harness (see also the manufacturer's instructions) and then is re-threaded through the figure-of-eight knot.

△ **4** To do this, simply follow the rope back through the figure-of-eight knot, starting with the part of the knot that is nearest the harness.

△ **5** When the knot is completed there should be a spare tail of about 30 cm (12 in). The rope loop now formed should be fist size and the spare tail tied to form a stopper knot.

● MAKING MISTAKES WITH THE FIGURE-OF-EIGHT KNOT

There are several mistakes which are often seen on indoor walls. Although many are not dangerous in themselves, they can lead to situations that can be either painful or dangerous, or both! These include clipping on to the main loop of the harness (if it has one) with a screwgate (locking) karabiner. Although this is still safe (providing it is a screwgate karabiner which is locked), any solid metal object next to the abdomen can cause bruising in the event of a slip. Using a screwgate karabiner also introduces an extra link to the system, which is unnecessary.

Another mistake is tying directly into the belay loop of the harness. Although probably still safe, it is not best practice. The main problem with doing either of the above is the tendency for the karabiner and figure-of-eight to get in the way and not keep everything neat and tidy. If everything is neat and tidy, you can see immediately when things are not right.

△ Tying into the rope using a screwgate (locking) karabiner attached to the belay loop of the harness.

THE STOPPER KNOT

The stopper knot is an important part of the tying-on procedure, ensuring the figure-of-eight cannot come undone while at the same time tidying up any loose ends of rope. Take the spare tail twice around the main rope and then back through itself. The trick is to get the tail the right length in the first place, about 30 cm (12 in), so that when the knot is finished there are no long ends to get in the way. This is not just for cosmetic reasons but for safety reasons also. A long trailing end of rope dangling down by the feet can be a real problem, especially if it is lying exactly where you don't want it, such as on a hold you are trying to use.

△ To tie the stopper knot, take two turns around the main rope, then pass the tail back through the turns. Finally, tighten the knot.

△ The completed "stopper knot" should be tight against the figure-of-eight, and there should still be a short "tail" of about 18–20 cm (7–8 in).

● MAKING MISTAKES WITH THE STOPPER KNOT

If the length of the tail of rope is judged correctly in the first place, there should be few problems. If, however, the tail is too long after the stopper is tied, it will not only look untidy but also get in the way and the climber may step on it if it's dangling by the feet. If it is too short, it will not form an effective knot. The only way this will affect security is if the figure-of-eight is allowed to work loose. This is unlikely in an indoor situation because you are only tied on and actually climbing for short periods at a time. The big difference comes when you move outdoors. Here you will use the same system, but in a different environment in which you may stay tied into the harness for hours on end. Therefore it's worth taking trouble to get it right! Always ask yourself, what happens if?

△ Doing it wrong: too much rope has been used, and the stopper knot is not snug up against the figure-of-eight knot.

Belaying and belay devices

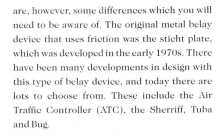

Until a few years ago climbers were still using the old method of "waist belays". This is where the rope is taken around the waist of the belayer and "paid out" or "taken in" round the waist and through the hands. The traditional waist belay still has a place in the greater game of mountaineering. However, today there are a multitude of belay devices on the market.

USING FRICTION

Although there is a vast range of belay devices on the market, most work on the same principle – that of friction generated by the rope being used to arrest a falling climber. There are, however, some differences which you will need to be aware of. The original metal belay device that uses friction was the sticht plate, which was developed in the early 1970s. There have been many developments in design with this type of belay device, and today there are lots to choose from. These include the Air Traffic Controller (ATC), the Sherriff, Tuba and Bug.

TOO LITTLE FRICTION

Some devices require a particular type of karabiner to give a smooth operation (you should refer to the manufacturer's instructions when purchasing a belay device); but, above all, it

◁ **1** *Here the rope is being "taken in" – the right hand is pulling the rope towards the belay plate while the left hand is pulling through the plate. Note the attention of the belayer to the climber above.*

▷ **2** *The rope is now in the "locked" position ready for the belayer to change hands and be ready for the next time that the climber moves (see also page 84).*

◁ Once out on the crag, your belaying technique should be "spot on" – whether you are belaying the leader or bringing up your second.

must be a screwgate (locking) karabiner! Devices which are easy and quick to pay the rope through to a lead climber are often referred to as "slick" and require an alert and attentive belayer at all times. This is because in the event of a fall, the rope will start to move very quickly through the belay device. The belayer will need to lock off, and effectively stop the rope running out, as quickly as possible. The slicker the device, the more difficult this will become if you do not act immediately.

PINCHING BELAY DEVICES

There are also devices that operate by pinching the rope to stop a fall. These work automatically – the belayer does not have to actively lock off. Because of this, they have found favour on many climbing walls. An inattentive belayer should, in theory at least, still be able to hold a falling climber. They also allow greater control when the climber is being lowered. However, it is very bad practice to get in the habit of being inattentive. It is a belayer's responsibilty to look after the lead climber, and this should not be taken lightly.

The belayer should always operate the device by keeping both hands on the rope and paying attention to the climber at all times.

Belay devices differ in their operation, but all come supplied with specific instructions, which must be adhered to.

● USING A GRI-GRI

The Gri-Gri has been designed for use at indoor climbing walls and on sport routes that are well equipped with bolts. Because they are less "dynamic" than most other belay devices, they should not be used on traditionally protected climbs – they will put too much force on the protection.

They are deceptively easy to use, but the instructions that come with them must be read and fully understood first. It is, for example, possible to thread the rope incorrectly through the mechanism. Also, when lowering a climber, the brake handle should not be used as a means of controlling speed.

△ The Gri-Gri will give a bigger jolt to the belayer should the climber fall off because it will stop or lock more quickly.

Bottom roping (indoors)

△ This climber is being belayed from below.

The most difficult job when starting out is learning how to operate an effective belay system. It is vitally important, because if you can't do this you will soon run out of climbing partners! Many climbing walls will have a section where ropes are permanently anchored at the top using a pulley system. The two ends of the rope will trail down the wall, enabling a climber to tie on to one end, while being protected by the belayer holding the other end. This is called bottom roping, because the belayer is operating from the bottom of the climb.

TAKING IN AND PAYING OUT

A belayer takes in and pays out the rope while the climber goes to the top of the wall and then lowers them back down again. The technique the belayer uses is called belaying and must be done correctly to ensure safety at all times, otherwise all the expensive equipment is of little use. There is a "live", or active, end of rope and a "dead" rope. The active rope goes from the climber to the belay plate via the top anchor, while the dead rope is that which is on the lower side of or below the belay plate. There is therefore a "live hand" and a "dead hand", which can be the left or right hand as occasion and position demands.

Belaying correctly from the start will develop a good technique for any climbing situation. It is important to keep one hand on the dead rope at all times, and in the locked position unless actually taking in, whichever belay device is used. Learn good belay habits from the start and follow the same procedure at all times. Also, remember to practise with your weaker hand.

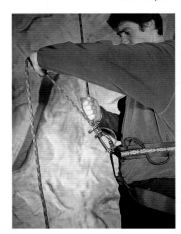

△ **1** Take the rope in with the "live" hand and pull through the plate with the "dead" hand. This requires good co-ordination.

△ **2** Lock the rope behind the plate with the dead hand and hold it by the hip to leave enough space for the live hand to move on to the dead rope.

△ **3** Take over the locking position on the rope with the live hand. You can then take the dead hand off the rope, move it up to take in the rope and repeat the same procedure.

LOWERING A CLIMBER

When the climber reaches the top of the wall, control their descent with both hands behind the belay device on the dead rope, creating as much friction as possible, and then ease the hands forward as necessary. When lowering a very light climber, it may be necessary to bring the dead rope forward slightly and decrease the friction. Devices like the Gri-Gri and Single Rope Controller (SRC) will need to be released before anyone can be lowered, but keep the hand in the locked position while the brake is released to ensure a controlled descent. You must refer to the manufacturer's instructions before trying out any type of device.

USING BOTTOM ANCHORS

Many walls now provide additional anchors or in situ belays at the bottom of the wall for the belayer to clip on to. This is particularly useful where there may be a big weight difference between the belayer and the climber. In this case, either belay direct from the anchor or clip a sling from the anchor to the main load-bearing loop of your harness to stop you flying into the air in the event of your heavier leader falling off – it does happen!

● GETTING IT WRONG

Common mistakes include loading the rope incorrectly in the belay device, making it impossible to get the "S" shape through the plate. This generates little friction on the belay device. Another mistake often seen is someone holding the "live" and "dead" ropes together in front of the plate. This will also result in little or no friction being generated by the device.

▷ *The belay device is clipped to the equipment-carrying loop and will probably rip out in the event of a fall or when lowering.*

△ *The climber is being lowered under control. The belayer is watching closely from a good braced position against the wall, with both hands controlling the descent on the dead rope.*

Learning to lead (indoors)

The natural progression after doing some bottom roping is to lead a route from the bottom of the wall, clipping the bolts (running belays) and the top anchor, and then being lowered back to the ground. Most climbers who are ready to lead will by this time have experienced a good deal of bottom roping.

THAT FIRST LEAD

The first lead should be completed on a climb that you are familiar with. The grade of the climb should be well within your capacity –

you don't want to frighten yourself too much on your first lead! There will be a continuous line of bolts (those running belays) placed every few feet on the route to clip as the climber gains height. Each bolt will have a short sling and metal snaplink karabiner on the end which the rope can be clipped in to. If your chosen route does not have these quickdraws already in place, make sure that you carry your own. You will have to place these as you lead the route, so make sure you take enough for each of the bolts. You should ensure that there are no twists in the rope or

△▷ Clipping the rope into the quickdraw can be done with either hand. Here the climber demonstrates, using his thumb to hold the karabiner and fingers to work the rope (above, right hand); and fingers to hold the karabiner and thumb to work the rope (right, left hand).

quickdraws as you make the clip, which can cause unnecessary friction or tangles. The best way to avoid tangles is to take one hand off the rock, staying in balance as you do so. Lift the rope from your waist and clip the protection by holding the karabiner steady with the third finger and twisting the rope in with the index finger and thumb. Always warn your belayer (they should be watching anyway) that you require some slack rope to reach up and clip the protection.

THE ORDER OF EVENTS

After checking your harness and the tie-in knot, climb up and clip the first karabiner. With the protection clipped, simply continue up and clip the next bolt with a quickdraw through it, until you reach the top. The belayer pays out the rope to the climber as they gain height and should be alert to their demands, especially when they need to clip a high bolt which requires the belayer to pay the rope out, take in as the climber passes the bolt, and then pay out again! Belay devices that lock automatically (such as the Gri-Gri or SRC) are not so easy to use to pay the rope out, so more warning must be given to the belayer. Lowering with a Gri-Gri employs exactly the same technique as all belay devices, but don't try and control the lower with the handle. The first few leads should be well within the capabilities of the climber, allowing them to familiarize themselves with the technicalities of ropework, rather than be near their technical climbing limit and unable to clip the protection.

Holding a falling leader will create much more of a shock on the belayer and may well lift them off the ground. In this situation you learn the value of using a ground anchor. This may take the form of a metal bolt in the floor or wall, or you may find a belay bag – a heavy bag to which the belayer can attach themselves. When the climber has reached the top, or they fall off (whichever comes first!), take the rope back in to the braking position, hold and control their descent with both hands and release the brake.

△ The climber has tied the figure-of-eight correctly, but the stopper knot is incorrect and will have to be adjusted before they are ready to lead the climb.

△ This is a "slick" device and it is therefore very easy and quick to pay the rope out to a leader, but will be a little more difficult to hold someone. In all indoor situations, the belay device is clipped to the main load-bearing loop of the harness with a karabiner.

△ This is similar to the original design of the belay plate. It is simple, relatively inexpensive and very effective. A fairly high degree of friction will be generated with this device so holding falls should be easier.

Using the climbing wall

There is no need to frighten yourself by jumping into leading when you first start climbing. Use the bottom roping system to get used to ropes, harnesses and belay devices. In this situation, provided the person at the other end of the rope is alert, the rope is positioned correctly and properly attached to your harness, there is very little that should go wrong. As soon as you reach the top of the wall, simply sit back on the rope while your partner lowers you to the ground. Falling off is no problem, because the rope goes from your harness, through the top anchor and down to your anchor person (belayer). You are able to climb in complete safety and this is a very good way to improve your technique, by pushing yourself with minimal risk. Finally, it is important to communicate with your partner. Keep the climbing calls to a minimum. Indoors you should require nothing more than the words "slack" (I want more rope) or "tight" (I want less rope). When the wall is busy it may be important to add your partner's name to avoid confusion. However, a full list of calls is included here with an explanation of what the call means (see opposite). The climbing calls are useful at the indoor wall. However, they become a vital part of the safety system when climbing multipitch routes outside. Communication is essential in this situation, but it is useful to become familiar with the calls early in your climbing career.

CLIMBING WALL PROCEDURES

When you are on a leading wall you will need your own rope, unlike in most bottom roping situations, where the ropes will be in place and it is normal practice to use those. All indoor walls will have their own system for monitoring and checking the ropes periodically. What you must do is establish what the procedures are when you go to an indoor wall, as circumstances will vary enormously. Something else that may vary considerably is the top anchor from which you will lower off. In most cases there will be a screwgate (locking) karabiner which can easily be clipped (and screwed up) before commencing your descent. Other walls may have a system similar to the lower-off points shown on page 94. This should present no problem as long as you are prepared, otherwise things may come as a shock, particularly at the top of your first lead!

▽ The first bolt is often the most difficult to clip but is also the most important. It will stop you hitting the ground in the event of a fall.

● THE CLIMBING CALLS

The call (UK)	The call (US)	Its meaning
Safe!	*Off belay!*	Leader's call to inform belayer (second) that leader is safe.
Taking in!	*Taking in!*	Leader's call to second that leader is taking excess rope in.
That's me!	*That's me!*	Second's call to leader, rope is tight on second.
Climb when ready!	*Climb when ready!*	Leader's call to second after putting rope through belay plate.
Climbing!	*Climbing!*	Second informing leader they are ready to climb.
OK!	*Climb on!*	Leader's affirmative to second, second starts climbing.
Slack!	*Slack!*	Pay out more rope.
Tight! (Tight rope!)	*Take!*	Take in any slack rope
Watch me!	*Watch me!*	Leader's call to belayer to pay attention during sequence of hard moves.

● LIVING DANGEROUSLY

Because of the friendly atmosphere of many indoor climbing venues, and climbers in the main being sociable animals, there is a tendency to be lulled into a false sense of security and to be a little casual. This has to be fought against at all times. One lapse could lead to an accident. Here are some common dangerous situations seen at climbing walls:

• Standing too far away from the wall when belaying. This is especially dangerous if the climber is heavier than the belayer, because it is possible for them to be pulled off their feet and into the wall, letting go of the belay device in the process.

• Allowing the elbow of the "dead" or locking hand to become trapped by standing with it too close to the wall. This could make it very difficult to lock off properly if your climber falls. You need to give your locking-off hand plenty of room to move.

• Talking to people standing around you while you are belaying. This is dangerous because it means you are not concentrating on what your climber is doing.

▷ *These belayers are standing too far away from the wall and are not concentrating on their climbing partners.*

Safety outdoors

Although the techniques used climbing indoors can be used outside on real rock, there are many differences that the novice climber should be aware of. These are not always obvious. Safety and self-reliance become very important in this wider environment, as do considerations such as conservation, first aid, navigation, weather and appropriate clothing and equipment.

● USING A GUIDEBOOK

It is important to have access to a guidebook. This will enable you to find the routes you want. Starting up the wrong route could quickly lead you into trouble if the route is harder than you expected! Remember that guidebooks have different conventions.

▷*Guidebooks often have maps, topographical guides and photographs to help locate your chosen route.*

THINKING OF THE ENVIRONMENT

Before looking in detail at climbing outdoors, and particularly the ropework involved, it must be stressed that the natural environment is fragile and easily damaged. All climbers have a responsibility regarding the countryside they enjoy and must ensure a minimal impact and help to preserve it for future generations. Follow the Climbers' Code and be considerate to landowners, property as well as others enjoying the outdoors. As climbers you will come into contact with hikers, backpackers and those just out for a Sunday afternoon stroll.

PERSONAL SAFETY

Even if you are just going bouldering, consider telling someone where you're going and, more important, when you expect to be back. There is a great deal of difference in climbing real rock away from the chalk-laden atmosphere of the indoor wall and many more things to consider, not least of which may be the weather! Remember that rock is a natural material and subject to weathering which will occasionally result in loose hand or footholds; it may be slippery and covered in moss and lichen, so take care, especially in wet conditions. The advice of an experienced person can be invaluable in these situations. The climbing calls are much more· important outside, especially on busy crags and on windy days on long pitches. A list of the calls and an explanation of what they mean is given on page 89. Stick to the list to avoid confusion and use your partner's name if the crag is crowded.

◁*This is an example of human erosion, caused by the passage of thousands of feet. It is a serious problem in some areas.*

Single-pitch climbs

Ropework in the outdoors follows exactly the same principles as indoors – it's just the environment that's changed! On traditional climbs, anchors must be created using wires, slings, hexes and spring-loaded camming devices (SLCDs) (see pages 98–99), rather than just clipping the bolts, as you would indoors or on sport crags. If the crag is situated at the top of a steep hillside, belays will have to be constructed before starting the climb. The leader will place protection (the wires, hexes, and so on) as they climb, create belays at the top, anchor themselves securely, then take the rope in and belay the second climber. All anchor points and belays require a sound judgement as to how safe or marginal they are. Sport climbs normally have all belays and anchors in place, which makes life much simpler. The following pages deal exclusively with climbs that have only one section of climbing from the bottom to the top. These are called single-pitch climbs. Routes that have two or more pitches are referred to as multipitch routes.

△ A popular single-pitch climbing venue, offering superb routes at every grade. The rock is gritstone, which provides tremendous friction for the feet.

● CLIMBERS' CODE

- A climbing party of two is minimum
- Always leave word of where you have gone
- Take care with all rope work and anchors and put the rope on as soon as necessary
- Test each hold, wherever possible, before trusting any weight to it
- Keep the party together at all times
- Don't let desire overrule judgement; never regret a retreat
- Don't climb beyond the limit of your ability and knowledge
- Always carry a first aid kit, whistle and sufficient food and clothing if you intend climbing on outdoor crags
- Check the weather forecast if venturing into the hills

△ Belaying at the top of a single-pitch climb. But how safe is a belay using snaplink karabiners?

Sport routes

There are many climbing areas throughout the world consisting entirely of sport climbs. All the anchors will (or should) be in place and fixed lower-off points will be found situated at the top of the climb. This makes life relatively simple for the climber, and certainly cuts down on the amount of climbing equipment that will be needed to deal with a route. You will need your harness, a rope, some slings, and as many quickdraws as there are bolts to clip on the route. You will also need your partner, belay device and some screwgate (locking) karabiners. The clothing you wear (see pages 18–19) will depend upon the weather and your preference. As you are on single pitch climbs, being caught out by the weather may not be as bad as being caught out on a much longer multipitch route. These routes offer an easy transition from indoor climbing.

▷ *This is a typical rack required for modern sport, or bolted, routes. It is well worth taking an extra couple of quickdraws and a spare screwgate (locking) karabiner.*

▽ *Many limestone crags are bolted because they are often difficult to protect in the traditional way. Limestone usually offers steep, exhilarating and gymnastic climbing.*

PREPARATION

Before starting, the rope should be run through the hands and laid loosely on the ground. The leader then ties on to the end of rope that is on top of the pile. This is important as it will reduce the risk of unnecessary tangles. If the leader ties on to the end of rope at the bottom of the pile, the rope will run out through the entire length of itself and may at some point create an unwanted knot or tangle. Now check each other's harness and knots. Climbing is about teamwork, and this is where it starts. The leader shoud clean and dry their shoes before starting the climb to remove all traces of dust or dampness – slipping off on the first two or three moves frightens you and doesn't impress your belayer! Do not forget to use the climbing calls either (see page 89).

THE CLIMB

The leader clips the bolts exactly the same as with indoor climbing. This will ensure that, in the event of a fall, they will not hit the ground! The belayer should remain alert at all times, paying out the rope when needed and taking it in when necessary. The bolts are clipped using a short sling, the quickdraw, which has a karabiner on each end. One karabiner is for clipping the bolt and the other is for clipping the rope. It should be possible to count from the ground the number of quickdraws needed, eliminating the need to carry excess equipment (although it's good practice to allow for one or two more quickdraws than seem necessary – there's the chance of one bolt being hidden from view, or you may drop a quickdraw in your excitement!). Karabiners with a bent gate should always be used on the rope and not directly clipped to the bolt. This is because there is a possibility of them becoming unclipped in the event of a fall.

△ This is a sport route. The next piece of protection is visible above and to the left of the climber. To reach that point the climber will rely almost exclusively on the superb frictional quality of the rock.

◁ Climbing calls may seem a little pedantic for single-pitch venues, but they are important on windy days and multipitch routes, so develop good habits early in your climbing career.

ROPEWORK

A fixed lower-off

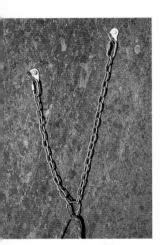

There should be fixed lower-off anchors in place at the top of sport routes. These will take the form of bolts or rings through which the rope can be threaded. You should always follow a strict procedure when using them, as any mistake could be fatal. You should also keep your belayer informed as to what you are doing, making sure that they know when you want them to start lowering.

◁ *These two anchor points are equally and independently loaded so if one should fail, which is highly unlikely, the other will not be shock-loaded. Having two separate anchors also gives some lateral stability to the system.*

THE STAGES

The stages you should take are as follows. Clip yourself to the lower-off anchor points using the main load-bearing loop of the harness with a quickdraw or sling. Now pull some rope in (you will have to warn the belayer) and thread this through the lower-off anchors. Next, tie a figure-of-eight knot in the rope which is through the lower-off and attach with a screwgate (locking) karabiner to the main load-bearing loop of the harness. The original figure-of-eight knot that you tied to your harness before you started to climb can now be untied. Now remove the quickdraw or sling that you used to attach yourself to the lower-off anchors. Inform your belayer that they can now take in

△ **1** *Clip a quickdraw between the anchor and main load-bearing loop of the harness, pull some rope up from the belayer and pass this through the "lower-off".*

△ **2** *Now tie a figure-of-eight on the length of rope you have passed through the lower-off. Clip this with a screwgate (locking) karabiner into the main load-bearing loop of the harness.*

△ **3** *The original figure-of-eight tied in to the harness can now be untied and taken off, the quickdraw removed and the climber lowered down.*

the slack rope and then lower you back down the route in safety. Quickdraws can be retrieved from the bolts on the way down and the rope can be pulled down through the lower-off ready for the next climb. Alternatively, the rope can be left in place and your belayer can bottom rope the route should they decide not to lead it. This is a fairly simple procedure, but must be adhered to step by step. Do not be tempted to take any shortcuts. Good communications should be maintained between the climber and belayer and shouldn't be too complicated. If, however, there are problems in communication (due to a high wind, long pitch or whatever), then you can resort to some form of hand signals or sharp tugs on the rope. It is as well to discuss these other forms of communication before you leave the ground, making sure that both of you know precisely what each gesture or tug will stand for. This goes back to the overall importance of communication when climbing outside.

● SORTING OUT PROBLEMS

Problems can occur when either the sequence of events you should follow to safely carry out a lower-off is forgotten or you don't have a spare quickdraw with which to make yourself safe when you arrive at the lower-off anchors. You can try and retrieve a quickdraw from lower down the climb to use, though this may prove difficult and time-consuming. The important point is clipping the figure-of-eight knot into the main load-bearing loop of the harness. If you were to clip it to the rope loop formed by the original figure-of-eight knot which goes through the harness, you would not be able to untie this original knot, which would at the very least be embarrassing. This is why the quickdraw is used to back the system up in the first place.

The other difficulty occurs when the route is longer than half of the length of the rope (say, over 20 m/65 ft in length), making lowering-off impossible. This is solved by belaying at the top of the route rather than at the bottom. This is called top roping, and is explained in detail on pages 104–117. Take care to keep a good belay directly in line between the anchor and the climber below. If there is a descent route it may be worth taking a pair of shoes suitable for scrambling down steep, slippery paths. Modern rock shoes are wonderful things but useless on wet ground! Alternatively, you could use two ropes to double the length of any lower-off that is required, though this requires a lot of ropework skill and thought.

Traditional routes

Traditional climbs do not have any fixed gear in them (in general) to protect the lead climber as they ascend the route. This is why the Victorian climbers had the dictum that the lead climber should never fall. The consequences were too high a price to pay. This may well have restricted many lead climbers of the day to leading routes well within the grade at which they could comfortably climb – although climbing outdoors on traditional routes can, and will, throw up surprises. The picture has changed considerably with the advent of modern leader-placed protection – nuts on wire and spectra, hexes and camming devices. This gear is placed into cracks or pockets by the leader and is removed by the second when they go up the route. What this does mean is that planning a traditional route in terms of the equipment needed is far more complicated than that needed for a bolted sport route.

GETTING TO YOUR ROUTE

Having selected the crag you want to climb on from the guidebook and decided on what route to do, you will need to get to it. This will

△ A traditional mountain rock climbing venue, where the leader places all the protection they need. The second removes it from the rock as they climb up.

▷ This crag is very obvious and only 20 minutes from the road. The difficulty arises when it comes to finding the route.

involve finding the crag on a map and walking to it (life is a little more adventurous outside!). This may take 2 minutes or 2 hours, but you will need the skills to be able to locate your crag and then the start of your route.

ON A TRAD ROUTE

The time has come to get the rope out and uncoil it carefully, leaving the leader's end on top. Put your harness and rock shoes on. Tying on is exactly the same as with indoor or sport routes outside. However, a big difference is that the belay plate is operated from the rope loop formed by the figure-of-eight knot on the harness, and not the main load-bearing loop of the harness. This is particularly important at the top of the pitch where considerably more strain will be applied to the anchor and belayer because the force is directly on to them and not absorbed by any other equipment. On traditional climbs both climbers should tie on to the rope before the leader starts, and if necessary select a good anchor if there is steep and exposed ground below the crag. Although this is not strictly necessary on some single-pitch venues, it will be on others; so if in doubt, follow this procedure.

SORTING OUT A RACK

The leader will need to arrange the rack of hardware on their harness or bandolier (gear sling) so they know where everything is very quickly. Placing protection on traditional climbs can be a precarious and time-consuming operation at the best of times. The last thing a leader will want, when strength and confidence are waning on an overhanging crack, is to be fumbling around searching for the one nut that will fit the crack and provide them with much-needed protection and restore composure! So, the trick here is to become familiar with your lead rack and know where everything is by touch and feel. Stick to the same order of racking each time you come to lead. This will save moments of blind panic when, as your strength fades, you become desperate to place a piece of protection.

◁ *The ground here is safe, so it is not strictly necessary to construct an anchor before leaving. The belayer is in a good position and able to watch the leader closely.*

△ *Here the belayer is still able to watch the leader but is standing in an exposed position and creating slack in the belay. The sideways pull could easily lift the chock out.*

△ *This is a much better position for any exposed belays. The belayer is tight on the anchors and sitting down. Note also the position of the belay plate in the rope loop around the harness.*

Constructing anchors

Protecting yourself and your friends on traditional climbs is an art that requires a creative mind and lots of skill and judgement based on experience. Everything that a rock face or ridge has to offer may be used. This will include cracks and pockets for gear, spikes of rock around which to put the rope or a sling, a thread, a tree (though there are environmental considerations here) and even the friction of the rope running over a rock surface. It is important that you learn the art of protecting a climb and creating safe anchors from which to belay. There are few short cuts to learning this art.

◁ *This is an excellent bollard, on which a full-weight sling sits comfortably. It will take a downwards or sideways pull.*

SPIKES AND BOLLARDS

Tying on to a large spike or bollard of rock was the original way the early climbers anchored themselves to the rock to provide some security for themselves and their colleagues. Spikes are still used but, as with all anchors, any spike should be thoroughly tested to make sure it's part of the crag. If it wobbles like a bad tooth, it should be rejected and something else tried. To test a spike, check it visually for cracks around the base and hit it with one hand whilst keeping the other hand on the spike. Any movement or vibration should be felt instantly. Alternatively, tap the spike with a karabiner and listen to the sound made. It will be obvious to what is good and what isn't. Any spike which produces a hollow sound should be treated with suspicion.

△ *Although this projecting flake is separated from the surrounding rock, it is still an excellent anchor because it is solidly jammed.*

● GETTING IT WRONG

△ *This anchor is poor because the sling is precariously balanced over a poor spike and any lateral movement could lift it off completely.*

△ *This anchor is poor because the sling is too tight around the spike. This will considerably weaken the sling. If a larger sling was used, the anchor would be good.*

△ *Spike belays are always very "directional". In this situation the slightest change in the direction of pull could result in the total failure of the belay.*

HOW TO USE A SPIKE

There are several ways to use a spike:

① Place a sling over the spike and clip the screwgate (locking) karabiner directly to the rope loop of the harness.

② Take the rope from your waist and tie a clove hitch to the screwgate karabiner.

③ If the spike is out of reach, take the rope from your waist, through the screwgate karabiner and clove hitch back to your waist. Alternatively the rope can be taken right around the spike and then clove hitched direct to your rope loop.

It goes without saying that all karabiners on belays should be screwgates (locking). Choose where you want to stand with care directly "in line" between the climber and the anchor. The clove hitch allows easy adjustment, so whenever a belay is constructed keep the rope tight between the anchor and belayer on all occasions, and adopt a good braced position, feet apart and knees bent. Most spike belays

are very "directional", which means they are excellent for a downward pull but can be lifted off easily with an upward pull. Bearing this in mind, they may be much more useful at the top of the crag (downward pull) rather than at the bottom (upward pull) if the leader falls off above some protection (running belay).

THREAD BELAYS

This is where tape slings are threaded in around two immovable objects, either a large boulder which is jammed into a crack or where two large boulders are touching so slings are easily threaded around. As with all belays, check the surrounding rock carefully because the slings are very thin and a boulder will only have to move a couple of millimetres to render the anchor useless. Thread belays do, however, have one great advantage over all others and that is the fact that they are multi-directional so they can be used in any situation irrespective of the pull. When the sling is fixed around the thread, clip the rope into the karabiner and tie in as before, either straight into the rope loop or using one of the methods with the clove hitch. The most important point is the position of the stance (how the belayer stands) and a tight rope between belayer and anchor.

▽ *The sling is taken through a small natural thread and both ends are then clipped together. The result is a belay that will take a "multi-directional" pull.*

● GETTING IT WRONG

◁ *This is a poor thread belay. The boulder is poorly wedged and a good heave on the sling will pull it straight out.*

Using lead-placed protection

Nuts on wires or spectra, camming devices and hexentrics (commonly called "hexes") make up the majority of gear used by climbers around the world to protect themselves on traditional routes. They come in a variety of sizes. There are several names given to some of these items (for example, nuts are sometimes called chocks, rocks or stoppers!). Leader-placed protection is usually placed in cracks. It makes excellent anchors for main belays as well as protection (running belays) for the leader while they are climbing. The function is similar to bolts on indoor walls or sport crags, the big difference being that the leader is using their own judgement about whether the protection is good, marginal or very poor.

PLACING PROTECTION

Each nut or hex (camming devices are dealt with on page 102) is specially designed to provide several options on which way it can be placed. They are also designed to give maximum holding power (using wedged shapes in the case of nuts and an asymmetric shape for hexes). Try and get as much of the metal of the nut or hex as possible in contact with the rock when you are placing it. This comes down to the correct selection of the size of the piece of protection. A general rule is to use the largest size that will fit the crack. Give a sharp down-

△ Slings, wires, quickdraws, cams and karabiners: collectively this equipment makes up a leader's rack.

▷ This is an excellent wired nut: well placed and with a lot of metal-to-rock contact for stability. The placement will even allow a good lateral strain to be applied with no fear of the wire failing.

● GETTING IT WRONG

△ Even though there is a lot of metal to rock contact, this nut is wedged against a loose rock and will take little strain.

△ This is a really poor placement. There is little of the nut in contact with the rock and it is simply resting on minute crystals.

▷ This large hexentric will offer a range of three different fittings depending on which way it is placed.

▷ This is an excellent placement and any strain will "cam" this hexentric into the rock.

▷ Extend wires with a quickdraw to keep the rope running more freely, particularly where wires are placed under an overhang. This will help prevent rope drag.

● GETTING IT WRONG

◁ This is a poor placement because there is little metal-to-rock contact – the corner of the hex can be seen clearly resting against the rock.

◁ Don't have wires clipped directly to the rope. This increases friction and may put a lateral strain on the protection and lift it out.

ward tug to jam or settle the piece of protection into place. Test each one in this manner and be sure to keep a good handhold when doing so, just in case the piece pulls out! Some placements will not be as good as others, but are the best available in the circumstances. As the leader, you will have to be able to cope mentally with this. The best solution is to find another placement as soon as possible that you feel is more reliable – this will calm those nerves and beating heart!

EXTENDING RUNNERS

All wired nuts and hexes must be extended using a quickdraw, otherwise they could be pulled out where any lateral strain is applied. This also applies to any gear placed under an overhang or in a way that the rope is moved out of line with the climb, creating friction in the system.

● RETRIEVING GEAR

The second retrieves all protection when it is their turn to climb. This can be difficult unless you have a nut key – a short steel bar with a hooked end which is used to lever or bash nuts and hexes out of their cracks. There is an art to understanding how best to get gear out, which only comes with time and practice.

▷ The natural constriction in which this hex is placed makes it extremely secure, so much so that it can take time to remove.

Camming devices

▷ A selection
of camming
devices that are
designed to work in either
parallel-sided or flared cracks where conventional chocks are difficult to use.

△ Place camming devices in the
direction they are likely to finish in
in the event of a sudden strain being
put on them.

▽ This is a large camming device
perfectly placed in a parallel-
sided crack.

O ver the last few years these have made a tremendous difference to the sport, particularly where any cracks are either very wide or parallel-sided and there are few natural constrictions to facilitate the placement of wires or chocks. There are various designs on the market and a variety of names. All have three or four cams that are depressed by pulling the triggers and then placed in a crack. They work well in cracks with parallel sides where conventional chocks would be extremely difficult to place. Some have solid stems and therefore work best in vertical cracks, but care must be taken in horizontal cracks unless the cam is placed with the end of the stem flush with the edge of the crack (see illustrations for more details). Others have flexible stems so they can be placed in either vertical or horizontal cracks with confidence. Try to find a placement where the cams are biting about mid-point, which is the best locking position for the cam. The geometry and direction of pull down the stem should ensure the harder the pull, the stronger the device. The closer the cams are to either fully open or fully closed the less likely they are to hold.

PROBLEMS WITH CAMS

There are several problems with camming devices, working on the principle of the more technical the equipment, the more problems there are, or at least are likely to be! Beware of "over" or "under" camming. The former can create a problem for your second when trying to remove the cam; the latter can be unsafe. If the rope is clipped directly to any camming device, the action of the rope moving backwards and forwards will "walk" the device deep into a crack, much to the annoyance of anyone trying to retrieve it.

● GETTING IT WRONG

◁ The camming device shown
here is very poor because only a
few of the cams are actually
working against the rock. The
front cam is almost fully open
and little force would need to be
applied to make it come out.
Cams used in "flared" cracks
can be good or almost useless,
but if there is no other option,
they will have to do.

The main belay

For a main belay use at least two pieces of gear which are equally loaded and independently tied off. There are several ways of doing this. Either use a sling to link the two anchors together creating a single point or use the following procedure: clip the rope through both karabiners and then back to a clove hitch on the rope loop of your harness – now clip the other (live) rope into the same karabiner with a second clove hitch. Use a pear-shaped (HMS) karabiner in the rope loop to accommodate both clove hitches and snaplink karabiners back-to-back on main belays if no screwgates are available.

Try never to use poor placements for a main belay. It needs to be able to take a potentially large force from a falling climber. Bolts at the wall or sport crag provide relatively reliable and frequent runners. A fall should not be huge. On traditional crags protection may not be so frequent so longer falls, which exert a greater force on the belayer, are often encountered.

△ This detail of a clove hitch clearly shows the "lay" of the rope (see page 111).

◁ There are many cases where it is not possible to rely just on one anchor, particularly if the anchor is a hex or wire. The answer is to link all the anchors to a single point.

▷ If your anchor is a single point, take the rope, create a clove hitch and fasten the gate.

▷ Any pull on anchors placed at the bottom of a route could be an upward one and is one of the major considerations when selecting an anchor.

• GETTING IT WRONG

◁ The belayer is not tight on the anchor. If a sudden force is applied to the rope, the belayer will be pulled forward and may let go of the rope or may shock-load the anchor.

The system

Arranging top or bottom ropes on outdoor crags has become very popular over the last few years, particularly where several people want to climb together. One reason could be that no one in the group is prepared to take responsibility or is competent enough to lead. Top and bottom ropes require less equipment and follow many techniques discussed in the previous chapter. If there are two or three ropes and two or three competent belayers within the group, it is the ideal way to allow beginners to "have a go" and try rock climbing. The downside to this is that arranging two or three ropes in one area could monopolize the crag and discourage others from attempting the routes. It is important to consider those waiting to climb the routes where the rope is arranged and it costs nothing to push the ropes to one side for a few minutes and allow others their fun, especially if they want to lead the climb. Top or bottom roping can be a little controversial and the complete picture is not here – this is just an insight!

THE TERMINOLOGY

There is often confusion among climbers as to the difference between a top rope and bottom rope, so here is an explanation of the terminology. If the belayer stands at the bottom of the crag or wall, they are bottom roping. They may or may not be attached to a

▽ Climbs at this popular venue will be top roped, bottom roped or led from the ground in what many would argue is a purer style of climbing.

◁ *This is bottom roping and, because of the relative safety, requires nothing other than the belayer to stand close in to the bottom of the crag.*

▽ *This is top roping where the belayer stands at the top of the climb in a direct line between the anchor and climber, and tight on the anchor. It can be much more difficult to hold someone when top roping.*

belay, depending on the exposure of the ground they are standing on and the likelihood of being lifted off their feet in the event of the climber falling. If the belayer is standing or sitting at the top of a climb, they are top roping. Because they are always exposed to being pulled off the crag, they must be anchored to a main belay. Climbs that can be bottom roped must be no higher than half the length of the rope – the rope must go from the climber up to the anchor and back to the belayer, who stands on the ground. If this is not possible, then top roping must be used.

In short, any climb of less than about 20 m (65 ft) should be possible to bottom rope; anything more than that will make it necessary for the belayer to anchor themselves at the top of the climb to belay.

Bottom ropes

We will start by looking at bottom roping, which to add to the confusion relies heavily on the top anchor! In fact the terminology, top and bottom ropes, doesn't relate to the ropes, as we have seen, but to where the belayer is positioned. The belayer is below the climb when bottom roping and above the climb when top roping. These terms only apply for single-pitch, not multipitch, climbs.

TOP ANCHORS

The ideal bottom rope should be established on a route suitable for everyone concerned. The rope goes from the climber's harness, tied on in the usual way, up through the top anchor and down to the belayer in exactly the same way as for indoor climbing. The only difference being the need to create a top belay. If there is easy access to the top of the crag, creating a belay should be relatively safe but do take care if it's slippery or exposed to strong winds. And always warn others before you throw the ropes down. The usual call is a good loud shout of "below" or "rope below". Bottom belays at the base of the crag will also be desirable, especially if the crag is at the top of a steep slope. Failing this, stand close in to the base of the crag just as you would indoors.

SPORT CRAGS

Many sport crags will have two bolts at the top of the routes so it's simply a question of linking these with slings and screwgate (locking) karabiners so the strain is equally divided and each bolt independently tied off. In some cases the bolts will already be linked by a small chain to a central ring and this could not be simpler. Clip a screwgate karabiner to the central point and clip in the middle of the rope. Always ensure any karabiners have the gate away from the rock and the opening end of the gate pointing down. This will ensure any vibration or movement will keep the gate closed. If the bolts are over the top of the crag, extend them with slings to just over the edge to avoid rope abrasion or erosion of the crag. Finally, double-check all screwgate karabiners are securely fastened. The other major consideration to remember is that a failure of the top anchor in any bottom roping situation could be catastrophic. The climbers' weight will also test the anchor when they are lowered so it must be absolutely secure.

◁ *This climber is carefully checking out the top of a single-pitch climb, with a view to setting up a secure anchor for either top or bottom roping.*

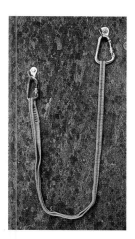

CREATING A BELAY

◁ **1** *To create a belay from two bolts is really quite simple. The two ends of a sling are clipped into the bolts with screwgate (locking) karabiners.*

◁ **2** *Gather the sling and tie a simple overhand knot. Keep the double-stitched part of the sling away from the overhand.*

◁ **3** *All the screwgate karabiners should be attached with the gates downwards. Clip the middle of the climbing rope into the bottom karabiner. This method keeps to the principle of equally loaded and independently tied off anchors.*

• POINTS TO REMEMBER

Many crags have "in situ" anchors and bolts, iron stakes or pegs (pitons), which are specially designed steel spikes that can be driven into cracks. If this "in situ" gear looks fairly new and well maintained, it should be okay. There are occasions, though, where some of this equipment may be old and in a poor state of repair, especially on sea cliffs where the salty atmosphere will have affected the metal. Always check carefully and don't trust this equipment implicitly. You don't know how long it's been there, who put it in or how far it goes into the rock. Treat all equipment you find in place on the crag as suspect until it's been thoroughly checked. Finally, if you are bottom roping ensure that the rope is long enough to reach the top of the crag doubled; some ropes have a colour change at the mid-point to assist with this.

◁ *The metal stake here is being used correctly, with a sling wrapped round the bottom next to the ground. This reduces leverage to a minimum.*

• GETTING IT WRONG

△ *In this example, excessive strain will be put on the stake because the sling is well above ground level.*

△ *This sling has not been secured around the stake. This may lead to excessive movement of the sling and consequent wear and tear.*

Using traditional gear

Creating anchors at traditional crags using traditional gear takes sound judgement concerning good placements of nuts, hexes and camming devices. Boulders, spikes and threads are often used as anchors and these too must be checked and deemed to be 100 per cent soundproof before being committed to use. Remember, the anchor you create in this system acts as a pulley and therefore takes around twice the weight of the climber using it. Creating anchors using slings, nuts, hexes and camming devices can be difficult to construct at first because of the inevitable lack of knowledge about what is safe and what is not. Because there will be a considerable strain on the anchor, it's vitally important to make sure it is safe.

USING SLINGS

Slings are used in a variety of ways. For example, they can be placed over spikes, threaded between two immovable boulders or around natural chockstones that are firmly wedged in a crack. They can also be placed around a convenient tree, but this should be discouraged as excessive use will eventually cause severe

◁ Here a sling has been placed over a large spike. The belay would have been improved if the sling had been clipped to the belayer's harness and the belay operated from there.

ANCHOR SELECTION

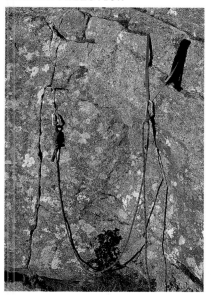

◁ **1** An anchor has been created using a nut and a spike.

▷ **2** The rope has been attached to the nut with a figure-of-eight and to the spike with a clove hitch. The anchors have been equalized using a figure-of-eight on the bight.

damage to the tree. If a tree has to be used, place a rucksack under the sling to protect it. Where two anchors are used, slings may be needed to link them to create a central point.

LINKING THE ANCHORS

Nuts and hexes can be placed in cracks and wedged to create an anchor. First look for natural constrictions within the crack and choose a chock or wire of an appropriate size. The trick is to get as much metal to rock contact as possible and settle in with a sharp tug. Never use one nut or hex as a main anchor – two or even three are always preferable. Link the two nuts with a sling (or the rope – see photographs above), gather the middle of the sling together and tie with an overhand knot. This is the simplest knot in the world – just form a loop and pass the end through the loop. Again, the trick here is to "equalize" the sling before tying the overhand. Using this method means that both chocks are equally loaded and independently tied off; in other words, the failure of one will not affect the other. With SLCDs find a placement with the trigger half depressed and the cams at about mid-point

and the direction of pull straight down the stem. Avoid if possible any lateral strain across the stem, although this is not important with "flexible" stems. Another point worth bearing in mind with SLCDs is that they have a tendency to "walk" deeper into cracks if there is any movement in the rope system, so extend them with a quickdraw to minimize the risk of this happening.

◁ The overhand knot is the simplest knot in the world. Take a section of rope, form a loop and pass the end through the loop. Here it is tied on the bight – a doubled section of rope.

Constructing a top anchor

There are some special considerations to bear in mind when constructing anchors at the top of a crag. Some of these relate to the fact that if the belayer is at the bottom of the crag, the motion of taking in and paying out rope will inevitably create some friction around the anchor at the top of the crag.

EXTENDING THE ANCHOR

All belays should be extended just below the top of the crag to avoid abrasion to the rope from constant rubbing as it is taken in or payed out. This action can also create erosion at the top of the crag, especially in the softer types of rock like sandstone. Where anchors are away from the edge of the crag, a spare rope can be used to extend everything to create a belay just over the top. To do this, tie a

▽ *Always pad any sharp edges to prevent abrasion on the rope. Use purpose-made rope protectors or empty plastic bottles, thoroughly cleaned, with the top and bottom removed.*

△ *Allow enough rope to tie a figure-of-eight below the top anchor. This will reduce abrasion and make for easier rope handling.*

● **GETTING IT WRONG**

◁ *Here, one of the anchors is not taking any strain of the bottom rope. All the weight is on one anchor. It is vitally important to equally load two anchors and tie them off independently. In addition, the belay is not far enough over the edge, and there is a danger that the rope will become jammed in the crack.*

TYING AND TIGHTENING A CLOVE HITCH

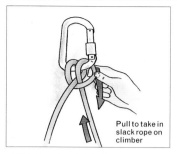

△ **1** To tie a clove hitch, form two identical loops in the rope and pass one in front of the other. Clip on to a karabiner.

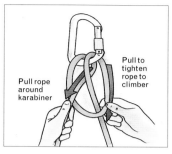

Pull rope around karabiner

Pull to tighten rope to climber

△ **2** Tighten the rope to the climber by loosening the knot in the karabiner. Pull on the rope as shown.

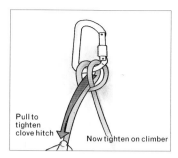

Pull to tighten clove hitch

Now tighten on climber

△ **3** Once you have the rope tight on the climber, you can pull on the section of rope to tighten the knot safely.

Pull to take in slack rope on climber

figure-of-eight knot on the bight. Allow a 1 m (3 ft) loop to drape over the edge and tie a clove hitch into the second anchor. To do this, form two loops in the rope, right over left and right over left, and slide the second loop behind the first. Place both loops over the karabiner. The rope loop hanging down the crag is then tied in a figure-of-eight. After the rope protector is put in place, a karabiner is attached to the figure-of-eight and the middle of the climbing rope clipped in the usual way. Check all screwgate (locking) karabiners are locked before descending to the bottom of the climb. The angle formed in the rope leading to each anchor should ideally be between 45 and 60 degrees, but should never exceed 120 degrees as this will increase rather than decrease the strain on each anchor.

● THE COW'S TAIL

Take a long sling and thread it through your harness and then back through itself. Clip a screwgate (locking) karabiner to the end of the sling and attach it to any anchor when you are in an exposed position. This might be at the top of a climb when arranging belays, for example. This method of attaching a sling to a harness (called a lark's foot) is perfectly acceptable for a personal back-up system. It must not be used where a severe strain may be applied.

△ The cow's tail attached to the harness with a lark's foot knot. The karabiner can be used to secure the climber to a belay.

● TYING A FIGURE-OF-EIGHT KNOT ON THE BIGHT

The figure-of-eight knot tied on the bight is a useful knot to know. It is used for securing a climber to the anchors of a belay and for creating a loop in which to put a karabiner on a bottom rope anchor.

△ **1** Take a 1 m (3 ft) loop or bight of rope, and double it back on itself.

△ **2** Take the loop behind the rope, bring it round to the front and pass it through "eye" in the loop.

△ **3** The figure-of-eight knot can now be made more secure by finishing with a stopper knot (see page 81).

Creating bottom anchors

Although anchors at the base of the crag are not always necessary or possible to construct, they are worth considering. This is particularly so where the climber is heavier than the belayer, or where there is steep ground beneath the crag and the belayer is not secure. Indeed, in this latter scenario, an anchor of some sort becomes essential.

CREATING THE ANCHOR
Anchors at the base of the crag are created in exactly the same way as they are at the top – using slings, nuts, hexes and camming

▷ In this situation the selection of a good anchor at the bottom of the climb is absolutely essential. Although the anchors here will not take an upward pull, they are the best available.

devices. Remember that the direction of pull from a falling climber in a bottom roping situation will always be upwards and not down. The anchor you make will therefore have to take an upward pulling force. A thread is ideal – it will take a pull in any direction. A spike, which is good for downward-pulling falls, may be useless for an upward pull where a sling might be simply lifted off. Trees also make good anchors, but there is growing evidence that they can be damaged excessively and will eventually die when all the bark is stripped off.

If the ground anchor is not 100 per cent trustworthy, add your own body weight by clipping to the anchor itself and belaying off the main load-bearing loop of your harness. In this way you are doing the best you can to improve the anchor, although you should still question whether it is good enough or not. If unsure, look again and apply some lateral thinking. It is really important to consider what you are trying to achieve when making your anchor. No two situations are ever the same, which makes it difficult to give textbook answers. Look around and get the best anchors you can and use them in the best way you can. If there are no good anchors, either belay from your main load-bearing loop on your harness or abandon the attempt and go elsewhere to create your belay, maybe doing a different route instead.

USING A DIRECT BELAY
If the anchor is absolutely secure, the ideal belaying system to use in this situation is a direct one. Simply attach the belay device to the anchor itself, using a screwgate (locking) karabiner, rather than to your harness. You have remember to keep behind the belay plate, so that you can lock it off successfully in

◁ When the ground anchors are absolutely secure it is common practice to belay "direct" from the anchor.

▷ One problem with bottom anchors is that when standing in front of the belay plate the belayer will have no chance to take the rope into the braking position. There should also be padding between the sling and the tree.

the event of a fall. Alternatively an Italian (or Munter) hitch can be used in the place of a belay device. It is less critical where the dead rope is held when using this. It is also very easy for a more experienced person to "back up" the system by just keeping a hand on the dead rope, thus allowing a beginner to learn how to belay. The Italian (or Munter) hitch is ideal for bottom roping situations, especially if novices are involved.

● TYING THE ITALIAN HITCH

To tie an Italian hitch, form two loops exactly like a clove hitch: right over left, right over left. Fold the loops together and clip both ropes into a HMS (pear-shaped) karabiner. The hitch is fully reversible and ideal for taking in or paying out rope. The friction is increased by taking the dead rope forwards and not backwards. Therefore the locking-off action involves taking the hand holding the dead rope forwards (not backwards, as with a normal belay device). This makes it an ideal knot to use with ground anchors, in that the belayer does not have to

stand behind the anchor – they can stand in front, which is usually an easier position to adopt. Never use a twist lock karabiner when belaying with the Italian hitch – the action of the rope can open this type of

karabiner. Use a screwgate (locking) karabiner.

▷ The Italian (or Munter) hitch can be used in a variety of situations for either belaying or abseiling (rappelling).

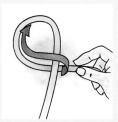

△ 1 To tie the Italian hitch, form two loops in the rope and fold them on top of each other ...

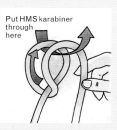

Put HMS karabiner through here

△ 2 ... as shown here. Attach the knot to a HMS or "pear-shaped" karabiner.

Climber ascending

Take in here

△ 3 The Italian hitch in action. The pear-shaped karabiner is essential, as it allows the knot to reverse.

Belaying from the top

There are many situations where it will be necessary to belay from the top of the crag. For example, if the climb is over half the length of the rope you will not be able to belay from the bottom. Instead you will have to create an anchor at the top of the crag and use a top rope.

EXTRA STRAIN

When belaying from above, you should be aware that a top rope will create considerably more strain on you, the belayer, should you have to hold the climber who is coming up from below in the event of a fall. There are two reasons for this:

① There is less energy-absorbing rope in the system.

② The rope does not run through an anchor (where some helpful friction is created) before coming on to the belayer, as it does in a bottom roping situation.

Any force applied will pull directly on the anchor and belayer, so it's vitally important to make sure the belayer is in a direct line between the anchor and the climber. The belay needs to be about 1 m (3 ft) back from the edge of the crag. In situations where there are bolt belays at the top, life is much simpler. Link the two bolts as described earlier (see page 107) and clip into the main load-bearing loop on the harness with a screwgate (locking) karabiner and lock the gate. The belay device or Italian hitch can be operated from the main load-bearing loop in the normal way but be warned: any force will be taken directly through the harness and on to you. This is a major consideration if the climber is heavy! Alternatively you can belay direct from the bolts and consider the use of a cow's tail for your personal safety (see page 111). Either of these methods will work in any situation where the anchors are near, or where you are within a few feet of the top of the climb and the anchors are 100 per cent secure.

If the anchors are 2–3 m (6–10 ft) back from the edge, use the system of clipping a figure-of-eight knot into the main anchor and clove hitching to the second anchor, leaving the loop 1 m (3 ft) back from the edge. The subtle difference here is that a figure-of-eight knot on the bight is now tied by tying a normal figure-of-eight knot, then pushing the end back through and over itself. If done correctly this forms two loops, one to belay off and one for personal safety. In this way the belayer is

keeping in position and belaying direct, and if the climber falls off the strain is put on the belay system and not the belayer's waist. Use a belay plate or Italian (Munter) hitch and the climber can either be lowered back down or finish at the top of the crag.

△ When creating a top anchor to belay from, try to find something of a suitable height above waist height. Sitting on the stance, as shown here, can help this situation.

△ It is vital that the belayer is correctly positioned. They should be in a direct line between the climber and the anchor.

◁ A popular single-pitch venue. There are literally hundreds of climbs at different grades. The rock is gritstone, which is a sedimentary rock similar to, but much coarser than, sandstone. It has excellent frictional qualities and good protection.

Looking at alternatives

There is very rarely a single correct way to make safe anchors. There are usually lots of ways to make unsafe anchors! The trick is to be able to judge between safe and unsafe anchors. You must always ask yourself what would happen to your overall anchor if one of the pieces of gear failed. Would a big shock-load come on to the remaining anchors? Would the entire anchor fail? In any situation, however you have made your belay, keep asking yourself these "what if?" questions.

THE TOOL BOX APPROACH

If you have understood the basic ideas behind building sound anchors and belays, you should be able to cope with most situations that the crags and mountains will throw at you.

◁ This is an alternative method of creating a single-point belay from separate anchors. The overhand knot is used exclusively to link all the points.

Remember that the skills you learned have to be adapted to these real-life situations. You will have to be inventive in your use of your own personal tool box of acquired skills to cope with the thousands of permutations of anchor creation.

TOP ANCHORS

In situations where several anchor points are needed to create a top belay, the overhand knot can be used in the system. Start as before with a figure-of-eight knot tied on the first anchor. Make sure you create the first loop just over the edge of the crag and then take the rope back through the next anchor, then back to the loop. When all the anchors have been included, tie an overhand knot in all the loops and clove hitch the rope on each anchor point. This will take a little practice to judge the right amount of rope required, but it is very effective and creates several anchor points to work from if necessary.

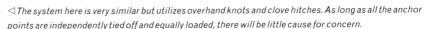

◁ The system here is very similar but utilizes overhand knots and clove hitches. As long as all the anchor points are independently tied off and equally loaded, there will be little cause for concern.

● USING A RIGGING ROPE

▷ Here is a good example of how to set up a bottom rope. A spare – or rigging – rope has been utilized to bring the main load-bearing point over the edge to reduce friction, erosion of the crag and wear and tear on the rope. The anchors are equally loaded and independently tied off so any force applied to the belay will be shared equally between the anchor points. A plastic bottle has also been used to protect the rope from any sharp edges there may be on the crag.

● COILING AND CARRYING THE ROPE

Many ropes are sold with a rope bag which incorporates a sheet on which the rope is laid at the foot of the route and folded around the rope at the end of the day. This is by far the best method not only of storing the rope but also carrying it to the crag. Another good method is to double the rope and feed two arm spans of the doubled ends through the hands.

Now take an arm span at a time and lay each one across one hand. Still holding the rope with one hand, take the two ends and whip them round the main body of coils. Finally a loop can be pulled over the coils and down on to the whipping. The two ends can be used to carry the rope rather like a rucksack, providing the ends are not too short.

△ **1** *Feed the doubled rope in coils over the hand.*

△ **2** *Leave some rope at the top to secure the coils.*

△ **3** *Feed a bight of rope through the top coil and loop through to secure.*

△ **4** *Sling the rope over the back and tie across the chest and around the waist.*

● THE OVERCROWDED CRAGS

There is evidence that a growing number of large groups are visiting the crags, and the rope systems described here are used extensively by beginners and groups. The main problem is that of monopolizing the crags. The popular areas are under extreme pressure and large, noisy groups can ruin someone else's enjoyment of a peaceful afternoon on the crags. Apart from all the technicalities, tolerance, an appreciation of your surroundings and consideration of others are important to bear in mind when visiting popular areas in a group.

△ *A popular climbing venue on a Sunday afternoon during the summer.*

What is abseiling (rappelling)?

▽ Having completed a route, this climber is abseiling (rappelling) back to the ground.

Abseiling (rappelling) is the technique used for descending steep rock either after the climb has been completed, or in certain cases where there is difficult access to the start of the climb. The rope is attached to a safe anchor at the top and a friction device, either a figure-of-eight descender or belay device, placed on the rope and attached to the load-bearing loop of the harness with a screwgate (locking) karabiner. By applying slight pressure with the lower hand below the device, a safe and controlled descent is easily accomplished. Some crags will have abseil descents from the top or in some cases, particularly sea cliffs, an abseil approach. In other situations, such as the onset of bad weather or misjudgement of the difficulty of the route, an abseil may be the only way of getting back down. In the early days of rock climbing, many primitive forms of abseiling were developed. On smaller traditional cliffs it is usually possible to scramble down the easy way. In alpine countries this is not always the case and abseiling is a necessity, particularly on the longer routes. The development of modern equipment makes abseiling far easier than it was but it is important to remember that any abseil is only as safe as the anchor, and that cannot be truly tested until you test it for real.

THE PERFECT POSITION

The perfect position for abseiling is easily achieved on a smooth slab with few ledges or obstructions and it's possible to see all the way down. A high anchor will make life much easier when starting the abseil. This is ideal for a beginner, but with more experience steeper, or even overhanging rock can be descended easily. The anchor must be 100 per cent bombproof. If it isn't, don't abseil! Just as in belaying, there is a live or active hand which is used below the abseil device to control the descent and a dead hand which is usually above the descender, although some beginners will want to use both hands below the device to control their descent at first. Keep the feet shoulder-width

▽ *The perfect abseil (rappel) stance*

Upper hand guiding the rope

Plenty of space between descender and back-up

Looking where going

French prussik or safety rope as a back-up

Body turned towards the leading hand

Lower hand maintaining friction on the dead rope and controlling the descent

Knees slightly flexed, acting as shock absorbers

Feet flat against the rock for a firm stance and shoulder-width apart

apart and turn slightly to the right if right-handed or to the left if left-handed. By turning sideways it becomes much easier to see where you are going and gives more freedom of movement to operate the controlling hand on the descender. The difficult part is committing yourself and going over the edge to start the abseil, but once that is done just feed the rope out and walk backwards down the crag. The feet should be flat against the rock and the closer you are to the horizontal, the less likely your feet are to slip. Flex the knees and control the rope with your bottom hand. There should also be a separate safety rope for beginners or a French prussik as a safety back-up for the more experienced.

△ *This smooth slab is ideal for practising abseiling (rappelling). There are no obstructions or cracks where a boot could get jammed. The ropes can be clearly seen reaching the ground.*

◁ *When beginners practise abseiling (rappelling), there should always be an extra rope used as a safety back-up.*

ROPEWORK

119

Abseil (rappel) devices

There are several devices that have been developed especially with abseiling (rappelling) in mind. They give a smooth descent and tend to dissipate the heat generated through friction very well. However, it is worth bearing in mind that most devices designed for belaying can be used for abseiling as well. It is a good idea to test a new device in a safe environment (on a short abseil or at an indoor wall) before using it in a more adventurous situation!

THE FIGURE-OF-EIGHT DESCENDER

The figure-of-eight descender is undoubtedly the best device for the job and specifically designed for the purpose, giving a controlled and safe descent. Harnesses which have a central load-bearing loop should present no problems; however, some harnesses require a karabiner to hold the leg loops up or clip the two parts of the harness together. In some cases this can "hold" the karabiner in place and possibly create loading against the gate.

The problem with this type of harness, sometimes referred to as a "Bod" system, is easily overcome by using a "mallion" (designed specifically to take a multi-directional pull) to connect the two parts of the harness together and thus create a central load-bearing loop. It is important to load the rope down through the eye so that it is on top of the descender when it goes over the back bar. If the rope goes up through the "eye" and under the back bar it could catch on a sharp edge of rock and "lock off" around the eye, thus preventing any further descent.

OTHER ALTERNATIVES

As mentioned, most belay devices offer reasonable options for abseiling and a varying degree of friction on either double or single ropes. The biggest problem with most (Tuber excepted) is a relatively small surface area which doesn't dissipate the heat caused by the friction during the abseil. In a series of long multiple abseils it is important to remove the

▽ *This is a figure-of-eight descender, loaded correctly with the rope over the connecting bar. Get into the habit of doing this automatically and always use a screwgate (locking) karabiner.*

▷ *With a "diaper" harness system, it is necessary to connect the two halves of the harness together with a "mallion". This is designed to take a three-way pull – karabiners, even screwgates, are not.*

△ This is a belay device which works very well as an abseil device. In a learning or practice situation it is possible to abseil on a single rope.

device quickly at the end of each abseil (rappel). Whichever device is used, it is important to always use either a safety rope or French prussik and clip this to the leg loop below the device with a screwgate (locking) karabiner. This is slid down the rope by the control (lower) hand and if this is removed (for whatever reason) the prussik should automatically lock. Where multiple abseils are involved have a "cow's tail" attachment from your harness to clip the anchor on arrival at the next stance before unclipping from the rope.

△ Tie a knot in the end of the rope before setting off. This may prevent you sliding off the end!

● GETTING IT WRONG

It is very easy to make mistakes setting up your abseil (rappel). To guard against this, make sure that you check your harness, abseil device and screwgate (locking) karabiner. A common mistake is to feed the rope up through the main hole of the figure-of-eight descender. If the rope is underneath the main bar of the descender it may turn in to a "lark's foot" if it catches an edge on the way down. This will lock the descender solid and necessitate a rescue, especially if you are on a free abseil and can't reach the rock.

△ A dangerous situation: the abseil (rappel) device is connected to the harness with a snaplink karabiner.

△ The common mistake of allowing clothing to get caught in the descender.

The anchor point

On sport crags, the anchor points are invariably good, although don't trust bolts implicitly, especially some of the ancient relics from a bygone age and always abseil (rappel) with care. The steadier you go down, the less strain there will be on the anchor, ropes and harnesses. On traditional climbing areas it can be much more difficult and the perfect anchor, one which allows the rope to be retrieved, is often elusive. In some cases it may be necessary to abandon a sling and abseil off this rather than risk getting the rope jammed in a crack. Trees often make excellent anchors but this causes serious damage when ropes are pulled down. However, if it is absolutely necessary, leave a sling in place and abseil off this rather than placing the rope directly round the tree. Many trees have been killed over the years by continual use, particularly by people abseiling at many climbing venues throughout the world. This is bad enough, but further damage will be caused to the crag when the root systems die, so use them only as a last resort. Choose a high anchor point, at least above waist-height. Having a low anchor not only raises the risk of the rope slipping off but increases strain on the anchor because of the outward directional pull on it. Finally a low anchor will make life difficult, and therefore dangerous, when you are going over the edge. Last but by no means least, choose the place to abseil with care, making sure that no one is climbing up and giving a good warning shout of "rope below" when throwing the ropes down just in case.

◁ Where there are several pieces of equipment to abseil (rappel) off, try and link all the anchors to ensure all are equally loaded and independently tied off.

▷ A well-placed nut will save the situation should the anchor fail. Note that the nut is not loaded – it is a back-up. If all has gone well, the last person to abseil (rappel) may risk removing it.

• GETTING IT WRONG

A very poor site has been chosen, especially for someone who is just learning. The abseiler will be unable to see if the ropes reach the bottom because of the extremely steep take-off point and low anchor. This will create difficulties as they go over the edge. They could turn upside down because of the direction of pull on the anchor. There have been a few cases where a hole has been punched in the karabiner gate, causing the system to fail. This is much more likely if an anchor point which is lower than the take-off point has been chosen, allowing the descender to flick over and pull across the gate.

△ *Choice of anchors for an abseil (rappel) is crucial for success. Here the anchors are too low.*

△ *A high anchor point makes life easy at the start of an abseil (rappel). The anchor is above the belay device and allows the abseiler to get the correct position before going over the edge.*

◁ *Never abseil (rappel) above a climber who may be leading a route. The last thing a leader wants is for someone to dislodge stones on to their head.*

The popularity of abseiling as the normal means of descent from many crags is due to the dislike of slithering down muddy paths in expensive footwear that is totally unsuited for the purpose. Abseiling is an essential (and inherently dangerous) technique to be learnt. There are many shiny gadgets on the market which are designed to make life easier, but none are of the slightest use unless the anchor point is chosen with care and due regard for the consequences of the abseil. Once you have leant back and weighted the rope and anchor, there is no turning back. The anchor must not fail! When abseiling, all climbers trust the rope without question, but remember the rope is only as good as the anchor.

ROPEWORK

Security

There are several ways in which you can make abseiling (rappelling) a safer activity. You can even abseil if you drop your belay device – using the Italian hitch!

THE ITALIAN HITCH

Although the Italian hitch is not ideal for abseiling it can be used in a situation where no other device is available, although in double ropes extensive twisting will occur. If the rope is used singly (that is, tied off at one end) the Italian hitch is much easier to use, although it still may twist alarmingly. It is essential to use a large pear-shaped (HMS) screwgate (locking) karabiner (not a twistlock type) to ensure the rope runs smoothly and to increase the heat dissipation. To create an Italian hitch, form two loops, right over left, right over left, fold the loops together and then clip the two ropes into the karabiner. The use of a French prussik as a "back-up" will make it possible to untangle the ropes. In spite of the problems, this method can be used in any situation where the abseil device has been dropped or forgotten. If using this method, ensure that the Italian hitch is operating against the back bar of the karabiner and not anywhere near the gate.

USING A PRUSSIK

This is a length of 6 mm (¼ in) cord about 1.5 m (4½ ft) long. Tie the ends together with a double fisherman's knot to form a loop; the loop should run from the thumb to a point level with the elbow. This is wound at least four or five times round the ropes, taking care to include both ropes if double ropes are being used.

Keep the French prussik short and snug and do not use any other prussik knots in this situation as they are not easily released once they are loaded.

Consider also how each device will be affected if the prussik is too long. In some cases the prussik will simply be released and in others it may be dragged into the abseil device.

△ **1** If you want to stop mid-descent (to retrieve some gear left on a route, for example), you can use the following method to free your hands.

△ **2** Take a length of rope around your leg for three or four turns. Make sure you keep hold of the controlling rope.

△ **3** Now carefully let go of the controlling rope. The wraps around your thigh should stop your descent. Your hands are now free.

Either way it could be disastrous and best not to find out, so keep those prussiks short and snug. There are of course some devices which are designed to lock automatically so a French prussik may be unnecessary, unless of course a malfunction (grit, dirt or inexperience) causes a problem in any way. In that case you'll look foolish if you haven't used one. An alternative way of providing safety back-up once the first person is down (or there is a responsible person already at the bottom) is to get them to pull gently on the bottom end of the rope. This should have the effect of locking off the abseil device and will not only give confidence to beginners but could save a good deal of time if multiple abseils are involved.

● SECURITY FROM BELOW

Today this is the standard way of helping beginners to gain confidence when learning to abseil (rappel). Good communication is important for both parties. Surprisingly little tension is required on the rope and with a little practice the person at the bottom can lower the abseiler (rappeller) a few centimetres (inches) and then lock off again. The same technique can also be used in a situation where a series of abseils is needed to get off a major climb. The first climber should go down protecting themselves with a French prussik and the second climber protected by the first in exactly the same way. This will speed the whole process up for both parties. If the abseil is an emergency one where the Italian hitch is used, the technique will still work although in some cases there will be a little less friction on the rope so more tension will be needed. The amount of tension needed will depend on the amount of friction, and this will depend upon several factors: the thickness of the ropes, whether you are using single or double ropes, the type of belay device, the weight of the abseiler, and so on.

△ **1** An alternative method of providing security for the abseiler (rappeller): the first abseiler down simply holds the abseil rope lightly.

△ **2** Should they need to stop the next abseiler from descending any further, they simply pull on the rope, applying tension to the system. This will lock the abseil device.

Contact Addresses

UNITED KINGDOM
British Mountaineering Council
177–179 Burton Road, West Didsbury,
Manchester M20 2BB

Association of Mountaineering Instructors
c/o MLTB, Capel Curig, Gwynedd LL24 0ET

British Mountain Guides
Capel Curig, Gwynedd LL24 0ET

AUSTRALIA
Australian School of Mountaineering
166B Katoomba Street, Katoomba, NSW 2780

Australian Sports Climbing Federation
GPO Box 3786, Sydney, NSW

CANADA
Alpine Club
PO Box 2040, Indian Flats Road, Canmore,
Alberta T0L 0N0

UNITED STATES
American Alpine Club
710 Tenth Street, Suite 100, Golden, CO 80401

Acknowledgements

No book would be complete without a strong team of writers who not only understand their subjects inside out, but have made decisions in everyday climbing and mountaineering situations based on that knowledge. To that end, the author has been extremely fortunate in having Nigel Shepherd and Neil Gresham as co-writers for this book. Thanks also go to Libby Peter for giving technical advice on many of the photographic shoots.

I would also like to thank all those who have either allowed me to trawl through their precious photographic libraries or assisted in providing specially commissioned photographs. These are Ray Wood, Mark Duncalf, Alex Gillespie, Nigel Shepherd, Chris Craggs, Tony Howard, Simon Carter, Graham Parkes, Nick White, David Simmonite and Nick Banks.

George Manley's clear and explicit diagrams have reached the parts that even these excellent photographers cannot reach.

I am grateful to the models Libby Peter, Sam Oliver, Edward Cartwright, Paul Houghoughi, Debbie Birch, Caroline and Simon Hale, Patrick (Patch) Hammond, W Perrin and Gavin Foster; and to Neil Adam and Roger Jones of Bethesda for the loan of historic climbing gear.

Finally, this section would not be complete without a word of thanks to Judith Simons at Anness Publishing and Neil Champion, who had the unenviable task of trying to tie up all the loose ends and deal with a crowd of itinerant climbers who insisted in disappearing to the four corners of the world at the drop of a hat!

The authors and publisher would like to thank the following companies and organizations for their generous help in providing clothing, equipment and facilities:

Troll
Spring Mill, Uppermill, Oldham,
Lancs OL3 6AA (for their harnesses)

Edelrid Safety Products
Shap Road, Industrial Estate, Kendal,
Cumbria LA9 6NZ (for their ropes)

DMM International Ltd
Y Glyn, Llanberis, Gwynedd LL55 4EL
(for their slings, karabiners, chocks, belay
devices and rock shoes)

HB Climbing Equipment
24, Llandegai Industrial Estate, Bangor,
Gwynedd LL57 4YH (for their slings,
karabiners, chocks and belay devices)

High Places
Globe Centre, Penistone Rd, Sheffield,
Yorks S6 3AE (for their T-shirts and sun hats)

Jagged Globe
45 Mowbray St, Sheffield, Yorks S3 8EN
(for their sweatshirts)

Regatta Ltd
Risol House, Mercury Way, Dumplington,
Urmston, Manchester M41 7RR
(for their fleece jackets and walking trousers)

Royal Robbins UK
16a Mill St, Oakham, Rutland LE15 6EA
(for their clothing)

Schoffel UK
16a Mill St, Oakham, Rutland LE15 6EA
(for their windshell and other waterproof
garments)

Sprayway Ltd
16 Chester St, Manchester M1 5GE
(for their windshells, fleece jackets and other
clothing)

Stone Monkey
Y Glyn, Llanberis, Gwynedd, LL55 4EL
(for their clothing)

Salomon Taylor Made Ltd
Annecy House, The Lodden Centre, Wade Rd,
Basingstoke, Hants RG248FL
(for their approach shoes)

Plas y Brenin
National Mountain Centre, Capel Currig,
Gwynedd LL24 0ET (for the use of their
climbing wall and other facilities)

Index

INDEX